MW01032543

"In a world where viole
is an urgent call to redis
peacemakers can Christ
intended. Dive deep into ____
of Christ and you will be changed, for good."

—**CRAIG GREENFIELD**, founder of Alongsiders International and author
of *Subversive Jesus*

"From Palm Sunday to Easter Sunday, what does Holy Week have
to do with peacemaking? I'd never thought about that before
reading *Fight Like Jesus*, but now I'm convinced the two are bound
together as Jesus wages peace each day and teaches his followers to
do the same. Read this book for new insight on Holy Week and on
Jesus as peacemaker. Read this book to be inspired and equipped
for practical peacemaking today."

—**APRIL YAMASAKI**, pastor and author of *Four Gifts* and *Sacred Pauses*

"A friend who lived through the Troubles in Northern Ireland told
me that the anger he sees in the American Christian community
rivals the animosity that existed in Northern Ireland in the 1980s.
Fight Like Jesus is a timely call for peacemaking in a period of escalating violence. In a season of rising homicides, mass shootings, gun
violence, vigilante attacks, and deep-seated hatred, we need now,
more than ever, this call for Christians to embrace our heritage as
forgers of peace in a world of division. *Fight Like Jesus* will equip
us all for the difficult work of peacemaking and reconciliation that
lays before us."

—**SCOTT BESSENECKER**, national director of global engagement and
justice for InterVarsity Christian Fellowship

"For those who think 'peace' might be mild or meek, flimsy or
weak, author Jason Porterfield unpacks Jesus' embrace of a radical
peace. Built on a faithful biblical exposition, this book inspires and
equips today's courageous peacemakers to fight like Jesus. Will you
put down your hammer and join him?"

—**MARGOT STARBUCK**, author of *Small Things with Great Love*

"In *Fight Like Jesus*, author Jason Porterfield takes the reader through the final week of Jesus' life and provides a powerful vision of peacemaking by situating it within his personal call to build a more just world. This relatable calling gives the book deep wisdom and thick theology in a world where many are searching for substantive discipleship. Through practical lessons for the everyday peacemaker, this book is equal parts commentary, guide, and communal resource suitable for congregations and classrooms alike. *Fight Like Jesus* will refresh one's understanding of both peacemaking and conventional readings of Holy Week."

—**ROSE LEE-NORMAN**, formation pastor at Sanctuary Covenant Church in Minneapolis, Minnesota, and adjunct professor of reconciliation studies at Bethel University

"Rather than requiring political manipulation or military conquest, the decisive peace that Jesus waged required self-sacrifice. In *Fight Like Jesus*, author Jason Porterfield takes us on an undomesticated, and therefore more realistic, journey through Holy Week that equips us to walk the way of the cross in ways that make for peace. I commend this book with hope!"

—**JER SWIGART**, cofounding director of the Global Immersion Project and coauthor of *Mending the Divides*

"Written as a compelling narrative of Jesus' final week of life and ministry, this book weaves historical context and accessible commentary in building a tangible set of practices for those who want to take peacemaking seriously. Many describe Jesus as a peacemaker, but few do the thoughtful work of unpacking what that meant and how it informs the vocation of the church. This is a great book for any church that desires to take a deep dive into the implications and invitation of Holy Week as an embodied extension of the peace that Jesus waged two thousand years ago."

—**JON HUCKINS**, cofounder of the Global Immersion Project and coauthor of *Mending the Divides*

FIGHT LIKE JESUS

FIGHT LIKE JESUS

HOW JESUS WAGED PEACE
throughout HOLY WEEK

Jason Porterfield
FOREWORD BY **SCOT MCKNIGHT**

Harrisonburg, Virginia

Herald Press
PO Box 866, Harrisonburg, Virginia 22803
www.HeraldPress.com

Library of Congress Cataloging-in-Publication Data
Names: Porterfield, Jason G., author.
Title: Fight like Jesus : how Jesus waged peace throughout Holy Week /
    Jason Porterfield.
Description: Harrisonburg, Virginia : Herald Press, 2022. | Includes
    bibliographical references.
Identifiers: LCCN 2021048949 (print) | LCCN 2021048950 (ebook) | ISBN
    9781513809342 (paperback) | ISBN 9781513809359 (hardcover) | ISBN
    9781513809366 (epub)
Subjects: LCSH: Jesus Christ--Passion. | Jesus Christ--Example. |
    Nonviolence--Religious aspects--Christianity. | BISAC: RELIGION /
    Christian Living / Social Issues | RELIGION / Christian Living / General
Classification: LCC BT431.3 .P67 2022 (print) | LCC BT431.3 (ebook) | DDC
    232.96--dc23/eng/20211122
LC record available at https://lccn.loc.gov/2021048949
LC ebook record available at https://lccn.loc.gov/2021048950

Study guides are available for many Herald Press titles at www.HeraldPress.com.

FIGHT LIKE JESUS
© 2022 by Jason Porterfield. Released by Herald Press, Harrisonburg, Virginia 22803. 800-
    245-7894. All rights reserved.
Library of Congress Control Number: 2021048949
International Standard Book Number: 978-1-5138-0934-2 (paperback);
    978-1-5138-0936-6 (ebook); 978-1-5138-0935-9 (hardcover)
Printed in United States of America

All scripture quotations, unless otherwise indicated, are taken from the *Holy Bible, New
International Version*®, NIV®. Copyright ©1973, 1978, 1984, 2011 by Biblica, Inc.™ Used
by permission of Zondervan. All rights reserved worldwide. www.zondervan.com. The "NIV"
and "New International Version" are trademarks registered in the United States Patent and
Trademark Office by Biblica, Inc.™ Scripture quotations marked (NRSV) are taken from the
New Revised Standard Version Bible, copyright © 1989, Division of Christian Education
of the National Council of the Churches of Christ in the United States of America. Used by
permission. All rights reserved. Scripture quotations marked (NKJV) are taken from the *New
King James Version* ®. Copyright © 1982 by Thomas Nelson, Inc. Used by permission. All
rights reserved. Scripture quotations marked (NLT) are taken from the *Holy Bible, New Living Translation*, copyright © 1996, 2004, 2015 by Tyndale House Foundation. Used by permission of Tyndale House Publishers, Inc., Carol Stream, Illinois 60188. All rights reserved.

26 25 24 23 22   10 9 8 7 6 5 4 3 2 1

To Mika, Luke, and Jono,

Throughout life, you'll hear many claim
that God hates the same people they hate.
But don't be fooled. God is love.
And God's love is most clearly seen in Jesus,
who refused to kill, yet was willing to be killed.

Contents

Foreword

The last week of Jesus raises a question for every Christian across all time. In fact, it is a question that spawns a host of questions. The gospel of Luke tells us that Jesus at least had a good idea, if not more, of what awaited him in Jerusalem. Whether it was because of his cavalier fellowship with those otherwise rejected by the religious authorities that wanted to control ordinary behaviors. Whether it was his seemingly egocentric claims of his relationship to God, indicating he was God's Son in a unique way. Whether it was his capacity to always turn the interrogations of his behaviors upside down into a deeper wisdom that unmasked the one asking questions. Whether it was his authority to permit his chosen few followers to break through the boundaries of the authorities' regulations of acceptable, worthy behaviors. Whether it was his undeniable ability to heal people and to liberate them from unclean, evil forces. Take your pick.

Those authorities picked a fight with him every day of that last week. He chose only to respond, and sometimes not even that. Sure, he flipped over some tables in protest, but he did not attack, he did not raise his fists, he did not fight. Author Jason Porterfield suggests that even the whip he used was limp. One scholar has said that in the last week, the lion of Jerusalem's powers opened its mouth and Jesus stuck his head in it.

His behaviors and words of the last week raise this question for you and me every day of every week: *Will the way of Jesus be our way or not?* Which raises questions like this: *Is the Christian way the way of violence?* And like this: *Is the way of Jesus the way of self-defense or the way of appeal to the powers and authorities?* And like this question: *How do you resist and disobey in the way of nonviolence?* If we don't ask this question, and these questions, we are not watching our Lord carefully enough.

Porterfield wants us to ask all these questions, and in guiding us through them he leads us day by day through Jesus' last week. You can't help but be surprised by how Jesus responded—and didn't respond. Porterfield opens with a stunning observation that I know doesn't register with me often enough: Jesus entered the week weeping over the city and its people as he says, "If you only knew . . ." His tears set the tone for the whole week and our every day. He entered that city with lament, unlike those who thought he was the one who would end oppressions and injustices once and for all. Porterfield asks us to think of the entire week through the lament of Jesus. What if we approached the powers in lament? Would we, as Porterfield says, learn to fight like Jesus? On social media? In politics? In cultural battles that seem driven by power rather than a compassion born of lament over suffering and injustice and the absence of peace?

Jesus lamented over the people because of their violence, and he knew this violence could not and would not bring peace. Ironic, isn't it? Jerusalem means "the city of peace," and here its forces were converging with violence while Jesus eschewed violence in order to bring the peace otherwise unattainable. Porterfield points at Jesus' understanding of peace as the flourishing of all relationships, and that flourishing is not spawned by violence. The descriptions in this book are breathtaking.

In his last week, Jesus celebrated Passover. Passover celebrated God's liberation of the children of Israel from slavery in Egypt at the hand of Pharaoh. Any celebration of liberation evokes hope and provokes acts of courage, and evocations and provocations are what the powers of Jerusalem most feared. No doubt some giving Jesus a big clap as he entered the city had such liberation in mind. But not Jesus. He rode a donkey to unmask the power of the armed horses of Rome, and he shut down the fanfare that emperors and tyrants conjure for themselves. Jesus was a dissident in his approach to peace. Power would not bring it. Or better yet, only a revolution in understanding what true power is could bring it. Only self-sacrificing love to the bitter end, the kind displayed in washing feet and in the new command to love one another and in a death on the cross for others, could bring his kind of peace.

Porterfield's *Fight Like Jesus* is an informed, thoughtful, reflective, and therefore show-stopping guide to Jesus' last week because, instead of gloating over the defeat of resurrection, it reveals to us the kind of Jesus who conquered death for the sake of peace. A peace attained not by might but by the way of the Lamb. I don't know Jason Porterfield personally, but I'm glad he asked me to read this wonderful book and write this foreword. His life and his book converge in these pages as a witness to the kind of peace we all need. I know

I do, and I pray you will put this book in your book bag or back pocket or on your reading stand and read it each day of Holy Week.

—Scot McKnight
Professor of New Testament at
Northern Seminary

Preface

The Failed Peacemaker

It all began on New Year's Day 2007, the day I moved into Canada's poorest urban neighborhood—Vancouver's Downtown Eastside. Though small in size, the Downtown Eastside is home to an estimated five thousand people addicted to drugs, twelve hundred people experiencing homelessness, and nine hundred women trapped in prostitution. It's a place the United Nations once described as "a two-kilometre-square stretch of decaying rooming houses, seedy strip bars and shady pawn shops."[1]

I moved to the Downtown Eastside because I felt called to be a peacemaker. That is to say, I believed God was asking me to work for the flourishing of this beautiful yet broken community. But I was young and naive. I hadn't done my homework. I knew nothing of the nightmare that had been stalking the Downtown Eastside for years. And so I was blindsided when, just three weeks after my arrival, the jury trial began in a nearby courthouse for Robert Pickton—Canada's deadliest serial killer. Over the span of more than a decade, Pickton would periodically drive into the Downtown Eastside, where he'd pick up a woman engaged in sex work, take her back to his farm, and kill her. By the time of his arrest, as he later confessed to an undercover agent posing as a cellmate, Pickton had murdered forty-nine women. Just one shy of his goal.

My neighbors were devastated. Pickton's victims were their friends—the closest thing to family many of them ever knew. My neighbors were also scared. What if Pickton hadn't worked alone? What if the killings continued? But most of all, my neighbors were angry. Indeed, they had every right to be. Why had the police been so slow to listen to their cries for help? Surely, Pickton would have been unable to kill so many people if his victims had been prominent women from the center of society.

The combination of so many destructive forces at work in the Downtown Eastside soon proved too much for me. The drugs were too powerful. The poverty was too pervasive. And the despair left my soul gasping for air. I had come to work for the healing and restoration of this broken community, but over the course of a few short months, my neighborhood's brokenness had broken me. Despite my claiming to be a peacemaker, it was now readily apparent that I had no idea how to make peace.

Perhaps you can relate. After all, you don't have to live in a place like the Downtown Eastside to know that brokenness is rampant in our world today. Maybe, like me, your heart breaks over injustice and you long to make a positive difference in our world. Yet you feel ill-equipped. You don't know where to begin. If so, this book is for you.

One day, a couple of years after moving to the Downtown Eastside, I dragged myself to church with what felt like my last ounce of energy. It turned out to be Palm Sunday, the first day of Holy Week. And as many churches do, this particular church turned the day into a joyous occasion. Children paraded through the sanctuary waving palm branches, the choir sang upbeat hymns, and everyone cheered "Hosanna!"

Everyone but me, that is. I couldn't bring myself to participate in the festivities. I was too depressed to celebrate. So when the congregation stood to sing yet another happy tune, I remained in my seat, silently pleading with God. "My neighborhood is in shambles, and I'm a failure of a peacemaker," I prayed. "Yet I believe you're still in the resurrection business, and that you continue to breathe new life into dying communities. So I beg of you, teach me how to be a peacemaker!"

Barely had the prayer left my lips before an answer arrived. When the sermon began, I decided to read my Bible rather than listen to the pastor's feel-good message. So I turned to the Gospels and began to read their accounts of Palm Sunday. That's when I noticed something that has forever changed my life. It's taken years to unpack the implications of that discovery. Yet as I sat in that pew all those years ago, I knew I had discovered where the answer to my prayer was to be found. If I was ever going to effectively confront injustice, call out oppressors, and contend for the flourishing of those around me, then I needed to study the Greatest Peacemaker's greatest week.

And that, dear reader, is the focus of this book.

1

The Key to Holy Week

A strange thing happened at the start of Holy Week. No one saw it coming, and ever since, few have noticed it. Yet it holds the key to understanding Jesus' final days.

At the time, Jesus was making his way to Jerusalem for the start of Passover. As he neared the holy city, a large crowd gathered around him, and when he passed by, they hailed his arrival by singing psalms, chanting "Hosanna!," and waving palm branches.

That's when the strange thing happened.

Amid all the excitement, nobody seemed to notice that one person was not celebrating. He was not rejoicing. He was not smiling. He was not having a good time. In fact, he was crying. The gospel of Luke tells us that while the crowd shouted cheers, Jesus shed tears (19:41).

Something important was going on here, for rarely do we find Jesus overwhelmed with such grief. In fact, the Scriptures speak of him weeping only one other time. In that instance,

Jesus cried alongside those mourning Lazarus's death. There wasn't a dry eye among them. But this time, on the outskirts of Jerusalem, at the start of Holy Week, only Jesus wept. What prompted this strangely dissonant scene? Why was Jesus crying?

Thankfully, we don't need to speculate about the cause of Jesus' sorrow. Luke records that as tears streamed down his face, Jesus cried aloud for all to hear, "If only you knew on this of all days the things that make for peace" (19:42, author's translation).

Like the weeping of a preacher at the pulpit, Jesus' sobs should have been impossible to ignore. And like a bridegroom's wailing at the altar, Jesus' lament should have abruptly ended the party. Neither proved true. For some inexplicable reason, the celebration continued unabated. Somehow, as improbable as it may seem, the crowd failed to notice Jesus' tears or to consider the reason for his lament.

I fear we have done the same.

Each year, our congregations commemorate the start of Holy Week by reenacting the crowd's actions. We sing upbeat hymns, shout "Hosanna," and wave palm branches with gusto. We've turned the day into a joyous occasion and filled it with festive traditions. Yet we never pause to reflect solemnly on Jesus' lament. And not once are we troubled by the fact that our emotions match the crowd's glee instead of our Savior's grief. It seems that like the crowd before us, we too have overlooked Jesus' tears and ignored his lament.

This is a tragedy, for when it comes to understanding the events of Holy Week, Jesus' lament is of the utmost importance. At the very least, it provides us with two crucial insights. First, because of this lament, we now know what Jesus was thinking about as he entered into his final days. And second, the passion with which this lament was spoken reveals the depth of Jesus' concern.

Taken together, these two insights teach us that at the start of Holy Week, more than anything else, Jesus longed for his admirers to know how he makes peace. Clearly, this was no trivial matter to Jesus. In fact, if his tear-filled eyes are any indication, making peace was his most fervent desire for the week.

What if Jesus' lament is more than just an intriguing glimpse into his innermost thoughts and desires? What if it was placed at the start of Holy Week as a marker so that it might guide us down the correct interpretive path? What if Jesus spoke these words on the first day in order to introduce his primary objective for the week?

This book makes a bold claim: Jesus' lament is the interpretive key to Holy Week. His lament suggests that the events of Holy Week are best understood when viewed through the lens of peacemaking. And it encourages us to see the central struggle of Holy Week as a struggle for peace.

Said another way, with this lament, the great drama of Holy Week began. And upon Jesus' speaking these words, the week's events were set in motion. For with this lament, Jesus launched a campaign for peace that would consume his final days. Each day, he would contend for our peace. And each day, he would correct the misguided methods we use to make peace.

THE MISSING PEACE

Admittedly, this is not how most people talk about Holy Week. You won't hear many sermons that speak of Jesus working for peace during his final days. And you'd be hard-pressed to find a single book on Holy Week that reflects on the significance of Jesus' lament. Few even mention it.

For years, I did the same. I saw no connection between peacemaking and Holy Week, so I simply glossed over Jesus' lament. Ironically, I now consider his lament to be of the utmost importance for the very reasons I once ignored it.

I used to brush past Jesus' lament, in part, because it felt like a random remark. His words about peace seemed to bear no relation to the unfolding events of Holy Week. After all, it was a very violent week. Priests championed death, crowds demanded capital punishment, disciples picked up swords, politicians ordered executions, soldiers delighted in torture, and—most startling of all—even Jesus grabbed a whip. Everyone seemed to thirst for blood.

I realize now, though, that we need Jesus' lament precisely because the week was so violent. Without it, our understanding of Holy Week is prone to err. Apart from it, the whirlwind of violence can easily turn us around in our thinking, dizzying our senses until we stumble out of Holy Week convinced that God is violent and that the cross somehow satisfied God's bloodlust.

My other reason for previously glossing over Jesus' lament was that I thought I already knew what it was alluding to. Sure, Jesus' original listeners were ignorant of "the things that make for peace" (Luke 19:42 NRSV). But I had the benefit of hindsight. I knew how Holy Week ended. And thus I assumed to know how Jesus made peace. In fact, the answer seemed downright obvious. It's the cross. The old, rugged cross. That's how Jesus made peace.

I still believe this answer is true. It's beautifully true, wonderfully true, foundationally true. But as I've come to see, it's not the whole truth. In other words, the cross was not the only way in which Jesus made peace. We need Jesus' lament, in part, because it warns against reducing Jesus' peacemaking efforts to just one solitary act. By speaking of "things"—in the plural—"that make for peace," Jesus revealed that his peace-making operation would be multifaceted in nature.

Without this lament, it's easy to overlook that Jesus was crucified on Friday precisely because of how he sought to make peace on the previous days of Holy Week. And if we fail to recognize this, then despite all our familiarity with the events of Holy Week, and despite clinging to the cross of Christ for our salvation, we may one day be horrified to discover that we've actually embraced a different approach to peacemaking. One that justifies killing enemies. One whose methods include nailing criminals to crosses.

IF ONLY YOU KNEW

Jesus' lament does more than just guide our interpretation of Holy Week. It also speaks a much-needed prophetic critique over today's church. For you see, I believe Jesus is still pleading for us to learn how peace is made. Tears are still streaming down his face. And he is still crying out, "If only you knew the things that make for peace. If only you knew how I make peace. If only you'd embrace my approach to peacemaking."

We desperately need to recover the radical vision of peace-making that Jesus embodied throughout Holy Week. And we urgently need to be trained in his way of making peace. The good news is, if you want to learn how Jesus makes peace, there is no better place to look than Holy Week. It's true that throughout his years of public ministry, Jesus had much to say about how to make peace. But Holy Week is special, for it was the main stage on which Jesus enacted all of his previous peace teaching. Throughout the events of that most sacred week, formerly abstract principles (like "Be merciful") found concrete expression, and lofty ethical ideals (such as "Love your enemies") became grounded in actual events.

That is why this book is both a commentary and a how-to manual. The remaining chapters walk day by day through Holy Week, starting with Palm Sunday and ending on Easter Sunday. As a commentary, each chapter shows how Jesus contended for peace on that particular day. And as a how-to manual, each chapter contains lessons—gleaned from the day's events—on how to be faithful and effective practitioners of Jesus' approach to peacemaking.

DEFINING PEACE

Before we begin, however, we need to identify what Jesus meant when he spoke of peace. Given the various ways we use the word, it's important that we not enter into Holy Week having projected our own definition upon Jesus. If we can gain a preliminary understanding of what Jesus meant by the word, then ultimately the events of Holy Week will further inform and refine our initial definition.

Raised by devout Jewish parents, Jesus developed his understanding of peace from the Hebrew Scriptures (generally equivalent to our Old Testament). There, a beautiful vision of shalom—which is the Hebrew word for peace—takes shape. Unlike how we often speak of peace, shalom denotes more than just the absence of violence. It indicates harmony, health, and wholeness in all aspects of life. Shalom exists when all our relationships are flourishing: our relationship with God, with each other, with creation, and even with ourselves. It is the state in which everything is as it ought to be, as God intends for it to be.

This vision of peace is profoundly comprehensive in scope. It leaves no aspect of life untouched. And it can never coexist with injustice. This is the kind of peace that Jesus labored to bring about during Holy Week. And this is the kind of peace that he calls his followers to also actively advance.

A SACRED JOURNEY

Equipped with this definition of peace and with Jesus' lament as our interpretive guide, we're now ready to venture into the sacred terrain of Holy Week. My prayer is that by the time we reach the other side, you'll be able to say, "Now I know the things that make for peace. And now I wholeheartedly embrace Jesus' approach to peacemaking."

2

Palm Sunday

Of Hammers and Lambs

The next day the great crowd that had come for the festival heard that Jesus was on his way to Jerusalem. They took palm branches and went out to meet him, shouting,

"Hosanna!"
"Blessed is he who comes in the name of the Lord!"
"Blessed is the king of Israel!"

Jesus found a young donkey and sat on it, as it is written:

"Do not be afraid, Daughter Zion;
    see, your king is coming,
    seated on a donkey's colt."

At first his disciples did not understand all this. Only after Jesus was glorified did they realize that these things had been written about him and that these things had been done to him.

> Now the crowd that was with him when he called
> Lazarus from the tomb and raised him from the dead con-
> tinued to spread the word. Many people, because they had
> heard that he had performed this sign, went out to meet him.
> So the Pharisees said to one another, "See, this is getting us
> nowhere. Look how the whole world has gone after him!"
>
> —John 12:12–19

When word came of his approach, throngs of worshipers poured out of Jerusalem's western gate, lining the dusty road, pressing against each other, vying for a view of the man, the myth, the legend, the great keeper of the peace himself— Pontius Pilate.

It was the start of Passover, the most sacred of all Jewish festivals, and Jerusalem was astir. Devout Jews from far and wide had converged upon the holy city to commemorate God's historic liberation of Israel from Egyptian enslavement. For a people struggling under the yoke of yet another oppressive superpower—this time Rome—Passover also served as a pain- ful reminder that they were no longer free. Year after year, the Jewish people came together to recall the time God won their freedom. And year after year, they hoped God would do so once again. With so many people dreaming of independence all gathered in one place, Jerusalem often became volatile during Passover. In fact, the week had a track record of incit- ing all-out insurrection.

During the Passover festivities of 4 BC, for example, a group of frustrated Jews enlisted recruits in the temple and then stoned to death a company of Roman soldiers. In response, the provincial ruler, Herod Archelaus, rushed his entire army into the city and promptly crushed the uprising. Three thousand Jews died, and that year's Passover was cancelled.[1]

From then on, Rome sought to prevent any future uprisings during Passover week. Peace and order were to be maintained at any cost.

That is why, as this particular Passover approached, Pontius Pilate, the Roman governor of Judea, left his coastal home in Caesarea Maritima and marched his army east to Jerusalem. As his procession neared the holy city, spectators lined the street and stared in wonder at the massive show of force. New Testament scholars Marcus Borg and John Dominic Crossan vividly portray the scene: "[It was] a visual panoply of imperial power: cavalry on horses, foot soldiers, leather armor, helmets, weapons, banners, golden eagles mounted on poles, sun glinting on metal and gold. Sounds: the marching of feet, the creaking of leather, the clinking of bridles, the beating of drums. The swirling of dust. The eyes of the silent onlookers, some curious, some awed, some resentful."[2]

In light of such power, all thoughts of resisting Rome were futile. Revolt was suicidal. Dreams of independence were crushed. Hope was deterred. Riding atop his warhorse, flanked by imperial might, Pilate knew that the mere sight of Rome's power had been enough to deter any thought of rebellion. He had won. Or so he thought.

ENTER THE CONTENDER

Suddenly, an excited murmur spread through the crowd. Then, much to Pilate's dismay, his onlookers turned around and hurried back into the city, as if they had lost interest, as if they had just received news of something far more entertaining to watch. At least, that's how I like to imagine what happened next.

For on this particular Passover, word came that another man, also endowed with power, was making his way to Jerusalem.

His procession was approaching from the opposite side of the city. The gospel of John tells us that the crowd rushed out to meet Jesus precisely because they heard he had raised Lazarus from the dead (12:17–18). If this man could raise the dead to life, then perhaps he had the power to defeat Rome. Sure, Pilate had swords and shields and chariots, but what power do such trifles have over a miracle worker who can control death itself?

All signs indicated that this would be an unforgettable Passover. As biblical scholar Amy-Jill Levine notes, with the two processions on a collision course, conflict seemed inevitable.[3] Jesus and his motley crew were approaching from the east. Pilate and his imperial army were advancing from the west. And Jerusalem—the city whose name means peace—would be center stage. It was to be the clash of the century, a showdown for the ages: Miracle Moses versus Egotistical Egypt, round two. At least, that's what the crowd expected.

And surprisingly, in a sense the crowd was right. An altercation was imminent. A war was about to be waged, though not in the way most Jews expected or wanted. It would not be a battle fought with fists and swords—at least, not by both sides. Rather, it would be the confrontation of two competing ideologies, the collision of two incompatible approaches to making and maintaining peace.

As the weeklong Passover festivities began, Jesus used his not-so-triumphal entry to showcase the differences between his approach to peacemaking and that of the world. The timing, location, and manner by which he entered Jerusalem all reveal profound lessons in how Jesus makes peace and, thus, how his followers are to also go about making peace.

But to see what Jesus' counter-procession can teach us about peacemaking, we must first take a fresh look at the crowd's actions. Only after we comprehend what the crowd was doing can we make sense of Jesus' response.

THE CROWD'S ACTIONS

As Jesus neared Jerusalem, the people who lined his path began chanting, "Hosanna, hosanna, hosanna!" (see Matthew 21:9; Mark 11:9; John 12:13). Nowadays, we use the word *hosanna* primarily as an expression of praise to God. It has become an interjection of adoration, similar to *hallelujah*.

But on that day outside Jerusalem, the word meant something far different. *Hosanna* is the Aramaic form of a two-part Hebrew word—the verb *hosiah* coupled with the emphatic particle *na*. *Hosiah* means "help us, deliver us, liberate us, save us." The ending *na* conveys a sense of urgency. When fused together, *hosiahna* meant "Oh, save us now!" or "Deliver us, we plead!" In essence, it was a cry for help.

That said, *hosiahna*—and its Aramaic form *hosanna*—often conveyed a secondary sense of adoration. When the crowd shouted "Hosanna!" as Jesus passed by, they were, in a real sense, heaping praise on him. But it's important to realize that the crowd's acclamation was a byproduct of their belief that Jesus was coming to their rescue.

The gospel of John goes on to tell us that the crowd recited a line from Psalm 118:26: "Blessed is he who comes in the name of the LORD." But then they added a few words not found in the psalm. They declared Jesus to be their king—"the king of Israel" (John 12:13).

Matthew's version of this event adds that people spread their coats on the ground for Jesus to travel over (21:8). Such an act may seem strange to you and me, but for those present that day, its meaning was unmistakable. Jesus' now coatless onlookers knew full well that this was the customary way to coronate a new king. It's exactly what the Israelites did, for instance, when Jehu was crowned king in 2 Kings 9:13.

Suddenly, this scene looks less like a jubilant pep rally and more like the start of a political rebellion. These people weren't simply celebrating the arrival of a religious hero. They were trying to make Jesus their king.

The gospel of John confirms this interpretation of the crowd's intent by including one additional detail. While both Matthew and Mark mention the crowd using branches, John alone specifies that the branches were palms (cf. Matthew 21:8; Mark 11:8; John 12:13). As Jesus passed by, John writes, the crowd waved palm branches.

Contrary to what church reenactments of this scene may lead you to believe, palm branches did not function as the ancient equivalent of those giant foam hands we see at sporting events. Waving them did not mean "You're awesome Jesus! I'm your number one fan."

In Jesus' day, palm branches were a politically loaded symbol that reminded the Jewish people of a significant historical event.

The Maccabean revolt

Roughly two hundred years before Jesus made his triumphal entry into Jerusalem, the Seleucid Empire ruled over Israel. In or around 167 BC their king, Antiochus IV Epiphanes, ransacked Jerusalem and desecrated the holy temple by slaughtering an unclean pig on the altar and sprinkling its blood throughout the place. Antiochus then ordered all the towns of Judah to offer sacrifices to his gods, and he sent inspectors to go town by town enforcing his decree.

In the town of Modein, however, the king's inspector met resistance. When one of the townspeople volunteered to make a sacrifice, an old priest named Mattathias stabbed the apostate to death, killed the king's inspector, tore down the altar, then fled to the hills. Soon after, Mattathias's health deteriorated. As he lay on his deathbed, his five sons gathered around him, and he said to them, "Avenge the wrong done to your people. Pay back the Gentiles in full" (1 Maccabees 2:67–68 NRSV).

Mattathias's dying words inspired his third son, Judas, to lead a somewhat successful rebellion against the Seleucids. In fact, Judas proved so fierce in battle that his countrymen gave him the nickname Maccabeus, which means "the hammer." Under his leadership, the Jews made significant headway in their quest for independence. Eventually, Judas the Hammer recaptured parts of Jerusalem, including the holy temple. As Judas made his triumphal entry into the city and proceeded to cleanse the temple, his followers waved—you guessed it—palm branches (2 Maccabees 10:1–9; see also 1 Maccabees 13:51).

From then on, palms became a key symbol of Israel's quest for independence. In fact, as the Maccabean liberation campaign gained ground, they started minting their own coins. On them they imprinted a palm tree and encircled the symbol with the battle cry "For the Redemption of Zion." Even decades after Jesus' triumphal entry, palms continued to symbolize the Jewish people's nationalist aspirations. During the Jewish revolts against Rome in AD 66–70 and AD 135, for example, insurgents once again imprinted palms on their newly struck coins.[4]

Given all this, when we read that the crowd waved palm branches as Jesus passed by, we must not envision this as a mere act of adoration. They were not simply praising Jesus. On the contrary, back then palm branches carried the exact same meaning as a separatist movement's flag does today. Waving them signified a desire to break free from foreign occupation. What's more, waving them at Jesus meant the crowd believed he would be their liberator.

JESUS' RESPONSE

Thankfully, Jesus was not caught off guard by the crowd's misguided assumptions. In fact, throughout his years of public ministry, Jesus often encountered people who pressured him to conform to what they thought his mission should be. In John 6, for instance, we read of a time when a crowd tried to make Jesus king by force. On that occasion, to avoid becoming the crowd's puppet king, Jesus employed a brilliant tactic: He ran away . . . as fast as his sandaled feet could take him.

As Jesus prepared to enter Jerusalem, he knew the crowds would assume he was coming in the likeness of Judas the Hammer to lead a violent uprising. So he prepared a response beforehand. In fact, Jesus' triumphal entry is one of the most brilliantly planned prophetic actions in human history. It was "street theater" par excellence.[5]

An unlikely prop

The first part of Jesus' game plan required the use of a prop; namely, a donkey. The synoptic gospels—Matthew, Mark, and Luke—inform us that earlier in the day, before beginning his journey to Jerusalem, Jesus instructed two of his disciples to procure the animal. Mark's gospel actually dedicates over half its account of the triumphal entry to this preparatory act. "This gives the distinct impression," New Testament scholar Ched Myers notes, "that all is being deliberately planned and choreographed."[6]

While the Synoptics reveal that the donkey was part of Jesus' strategy from the beginning, John's account focuses on the precise timing of when Jesus actually used the animal. The decisive moment came at the height of when the crowds were proclaiming their expectation that Jesus would lead an armed revolt. According to John, when Jesus heard the crowd shouting "Hosanna!" and calling him their king, and when he saw them waving palm branches and laying down their coats, that is when, in response to what the crowd was doing, Jesus decided to ride the animal (12:12–14).

Jesus' use of a donkey at this point in his procession accomplished two goals. First, it confirmed that he was indeed a king. When Jesus sent his disciples to procure the animal, he instructed them to tell the donkey's owner, "The Lord needs it" (Mark 11:3). By acquiring a donkey in this way, Jesus was "claim[ing] the right of kings, known throughout antiquity, to requisition modes of transport."[7] By using a donkey that no one else had ever ridden (Luke 19:30) and by allowing his disciples to set him on the animal (v. 35), Jesus was engaging in a custom reserved for kings. That, for instance, is what the Israelites did when Solomon was installed upon the throne (1 Kings 1:33–34).

Second, Jesus' use of a donkey also challenged the people's misconception of his kingly mission. Traditionally, whenever a ruler triumphantly entered a city, he would ride a horse if his intentions were warlike or a donkey if he came peaceably. Thus, as biblical scholar J. F. Coakley writes, "By not riding a horse, as a nationalistic messiah would be expected to do, Jesus intended to rebuke or correct the aspirations of those who acclaimed him. He was acting out the role of a humble, peaceable king."[8]

The crowd would have known that Jesus' use of a donkey symbolized his peaceful intentions. But evidently, they assumed this meant Jesus was coming to wage peace solely on their behalf. The donkey simply confirmed their deeply ingrained belief that Jesus would win their peace by bringing a hammer down upon the Romans.

It wasn't just the crowds who thought this way. Jesus' disciples also failed to comprehend why he chose to ride a donkey. According to John, the disciples only understood its significance after Jesus' resurrection (12:14–16).

Thankfully, John connects the dots for his readers. By riding a donkey, John explains, Jesus was aligning himself with Zechariah's vision of a peaceable king. "Do not be afraid, Daughter Zion," Zechariah prophesied, "see, your king is coming, seated on a donkey's colt" (John 12:15, quoting Zechariah 9:9). The next verse of Zechariah's vision goes on to say that this king "will take away the chariots from Ephraim and the warhorses from Jerusalem, and the battle bow will be broken. He will proclaim peace to the nations. His rule will extend from sea to sea and from the River to the ends of the earth" (9:10).

It's easy to overlook just how radical a description Zechariah offers of the coming king. Note, for instance, that this king will remove the chariots, warhorses, and battle bows from Jerusalem and the Israelite tribe of Ephraim. In other words, he will destroy his own people's weapons of war. Israel's tools of death will be no more. Zechariah's prophecy also states that this king will proclaim peace to all nations. Everyone will be beneficiaries of his peace, for his peaceful reign will "extend from sea to sea," even "to the ends of the earth" (9:10).

A symbolic setting

While the riding of a donkey was a profoundly symbolic act, it wasn't the only way that Jesus purposefully shaped his triumphal entry to advance our understanding of peacemaking. The

timing and location that Jesus chose for this event also point
us to his way of making peace.

As we know, Jesus made his way into Jerusalem on the
first day of Passover. It was a Sunday in early spring around
the year AD 30. More specifically, it was the tenth day of the
Jewish month of Nisan. This was the day when every family
selected its lamb as God commanded Moses in Exodus 12:3:
"Tell the whole community of Israel that on the tenth day
of this month each man is to take a lamb for his family, one
for each household." According to Jewish historians, the sheep
were supplied from Bethlehem and brought in through the
city's northeast gate, which was known as the Sheep Gate.

So too Jesus, who was born in Bethlehem, made his triumphal entry on the day when suppliers brought their lambs
into Jerusalem for worshipers to select. As Jesus descended the
Mount of Olives, his route into the holy city joined up with
the route traveled by the sacrificial sheep, and he likely entered
through the same gate.

As prescribed in the Torah, each household was instructed
to "take care of [their lamb] until the fourteenth day of the
month, when all the members of the community of Israel must
slaughter them at twilight" (Exodus 12:6). This gave each
household four days to inspect their chosen lamb in order to
ensure it was without blemish, for only a spotless lamb could
be slaughtered.

As we'll come to see, Jesus deliberately spent most of the
next four days in the public eye. During that time, he taught
openly and fielded people's questions. Again and again, he
corrected misguided assumptions about himself and dispelled
errant beliefs about his mission. Put simply, Jesus spent the
next four days under close examination, offering himself up as
the ultimate Paschal Lamb.

LESSONS IN PEACEMAKING

Now that we've identified how Jesus fashioned his triumphal entry to serve as a corrective to the crowd's expectations of him, let's shift gears and consider what the day can teach us about Jesus' approach to peacemaking. In future chapters, these peacemaking lessons will be interspersed throughout. But for this day, it makes the most sense to place these lessons all together at the end of the chapter.

As I see it, Palm Sunday teaches us three crucial peacemaking lessons:

Lesson 1: Christlike peacemakers move toward conflict.

The first lesson is that instead of running from conflict, Christlike peacemakers boldly move toward it. They don't ignore it. They don't hide from it. They don't pretend it doesn't exist. Rather, they willingly go where the need for just change is greatest.

On the first day of Holy Week, Jesus rode into Jerusalem knowing full well that confrontation awaited him there. Before the start of Passover, Jesus pulled his disciples aside and warned them, "We are going up to Jerusalem, and everything that is written by the prophets about the Son of Man will be fulfilled. He will be delivered over to the Gentiles. They will mock him, insult him and spit on him; they will flog him and kill him. On the third day he will rise again" (Luke 18:31–33).

If we are to become practitioners of Jesus' approach to peacemaking, then we must be willing to enter into conflict. We must seek out those places where God's shalom is painfully absent. Or, to adopt imagery Jesus used elsewhere, we must become like salt rubbed into the moral decay of society. We must become like light shining in the darkness.

This approach to peacemaking is not safe. It involves great personal sacrifice. Moving toward conflict required Jesus to abandon comfort and security. He could have dabbled in peacemaking from a safe distance. He could have kept danger an arm's length away. He could have remained detached from the conflict. Instead, Jesus became personally invested. He calls his followers to do the same.

Lesson 2: Christlike peacemakers extend peace to all people.

The second lesson that Jesus' triumphal entry teaches us is that we must work for the peace of all people, not just some. Christlike peacemakers don't win peace for their group by stripping it from another. Nor do they maintain peace for their side through the suppression of others. Rather, Christlike peacemakers are concerned for the well-being of all—friend and foe, ally and enemy.

By identifying himself as Zechariah's peaceable king, Jesus revealed that he was interested in more than just the flourishing of his own group. We know from Zechariah's vision that Jesus came to speak peace to all nations (9:10).

But if all people were to be beneficiaries of Jesus' peace, then such peace could not be attained through the world's usual means. It could not be achieved through force, for only one side wins when peace is pursued through violence. The weapons of war cannot build a peaceful world for all; their purpose is to bring about destruction. They are instruments of death, not life. They are tools that harm, not heal.

As Zechariah predicted, Jesus rode into Jerusalem intent on removing the weapons of war. He would take away the battle bow, chariot, and warhorse. And in their stead, he modeled a new way of making peace.

Lesson 3: Christlike peacemakers follow the way of the Lamb.
If we are to become apprentices of Jesus' approach to peace-making, then we must embrace the way of the Lamb and reject the way of the hammer.

Palm Sunday is fundamentally about the collision of two competing approaches to peacemaking. Given the theatrics of the day, it would be easy to conclude that these conflicting ideologies were embodied by Pilate and Jesus. After all, their processions were on a collision course, and everything about Jesus' procession seemed to deliberately counter Pilate's.

While this is true, Jesus also intentionally subverted his own people's paradigm for peacemaking. They expected Jesus to ride into town as Judas Maccabeus had once done. They hoped Jesus would wage peace with a hammer. But Jesus flipped the script.

Though they were enemies, Jesus' admirers and Pilate's army both believed in the power of the hammer to construct peace. They believed the making and maintaining of peace was achieved with force. Both parties embraced the world's approach to peacemaking, and Jesus was confronting it head-on.

Jesus used his triumphal entry to subtly yet unambiguously declare that he was not the Hammer of God. He was the Lamb of God. And he calls his followers to also embrace the way of a sacrificial lamb.

We will discover more of what it looks like to make peace in this way as the week unfolds. But as we move into the second day of Holy Week, we'll look next at an event where Jesus' actions seem to undermine everything he just taught about making peace. For tomorrow, Jesus will arm himself with a whip.

3

Monday

The Whip of Christ

In the temple courts [Jesus] found people selling cattle, sheep and doves, and others sitting at tables exchanging money. So he made a whip out of cords, and drove all from the temple courts, both sheep and cattle; he scattered the coins of the money changers and overturned their tables. To those who sold doves he said, "Get these out of here! Stop turning my Father's house into a market!" His disciples remembered that it is written: "Zeal for your house will consume me."

The Jews then responded to him, "What sign can you show us to prove your authority to do all this?"

Jesus answered them, "Destroy this temple, and I will raise it again in three days."

They replied, "It has taken forty-six years to build this temple, and you are going to raise it in three days?" But the temple he had spoken of was his body. After he was raised from the dead, his disciples recalled what he had

said. Then they believed the scripture and the words that
Jesus had spoken.

—John 2:14–22[1]

Say goodbye to the nice, kind, gentle Jesus of Palm Sunday. Prepare to meet the angry, aggressive, violent Jesus
of Holy Monday. At least, that's what the usual depiction of
Monday's events would lead us to believe. Gone is the one, we
are told, who said just yesterday that he'd extend peace to all
nations and remove the weapons of war. Today we supposedly
find Jesus disrupting the peace as he wields a weapon.

Maybe he had a bad night's sleep. Maybe the disciples got
under his skin. Or perhaps the constant back-and-forth trek
between Bethany and Jerusalem wore him down. Who knows
what angered Jesus. All that can be said for sure is that upon
entering the temple, Jesus lost any semblance of restraint.
Something caused him to fly off the handle, or—as I suppose
you could say—to have one massive temple tantrum.

In an instant, it appears that Jesus transformed from a meek
Mahatma Gandhi–like figure into a modern-day action hero.
Like Bruce Lee, Jesus singlehandedly overpowered everyone.
Like Indiana Jones, he whipped all who got in his way. And
like Robin Hood, Jesus confiscated the rich's loot and poured
it out for the poor to reclaim.

The hour for mercy had passed. Judgment day had arrived.
And Jesus, it turns out, was no wimp. He didn't need a host
of angels to help fight his battles. Armed with a simple whip,
Jesus defeated the whole temple establishment. None could
escape his reach. And none were spared his wrath. Men and
women alike writhed in agony as blow after blow of his whip
lashed their flesh raw.

Of course, there's just one problem with this portrayal of Jesus' temple action:

It's wrong. Pure fiction.

It's not just a slightly embellished version of an otherwise accurate retelling of the event. This is not, apart from the inclusion of some theatrical flair, a faithful summary of the gospel record. It's just plain wrong.

Despite the inaccuracy of this portrayal, artists have promoted this violent version of the temple cleansing for centuries. Daniel Dombrowski, who studied this event's artistic history, notes that "none of the listings of the temple cleansing in the standard reference work, *World Painting Index*, offers us a portrayal of the event where Jesus is not violent."[2] From Jacopo Bassano depicting Jesus whipping a woman to El Greco painting a knot of human bodies writhing in pain to Rembrandt's famous portrayal of Jesus lashing four horrified victims, the artistic retelling of this event is astonishingly consistent in its insistence that Jesus violently hurt people.

The result of such a portrayal is that many Christians have found a convenient way to justify their own violent intentions. If Jesus hurt people with a whip, so the argument goes, then under the right conditions his followers may also use force. Of course, those conditions are rarely identified. Instead, Christians have all too often divorced Jesus' actions from the issues that upset him, thus giving themselves free rein to respond violently in any situation. And by classifying the whip as a weapon, they've concluded that any weapon may be used, even ones infinitely more lethal and indiscriminate than a whip.

Indeed, the church has a long and checkered history of latching on to this image of a whip-wielding Jesus and using it to justify horrendous acts of violence. In the fifth century,

Saint Augustine defended killing heretics by stating that in the temple incident, "we find . . . Christ a persecutor [who] bodily persecuted those whom he expelled from the temple."[3] Saint Bernard of Clairvaux encouraged the Knights Templar of the Second Crusade to "go forth confidently and repel the foes of Christ, . . . [for] our leader himself armed his most holy hands . . . with a whip."[4] Even the great Protestant reformer John Calvin used this incident to justify executing Michael Servetus. "Jesus' meekness," Calvin concluded, "was not intended for the obstinate and evil."[5]

If you understand Jesus to be the Prince of Peace and not the Slayer of Sinners, then his actions in the temple can be quite disorienting. After all, the gospel accounts of this event—or at least the way many of us have been taught to read them—seem to contradict the Bible's otherwise coherent depiction of a peaceful, enemy-loving Jesus. Not knowing what else to do, many steer clear of these texts as if the whole event were spiritually toxic. That's unfortunate.

The gospel writers never intended for us to avoid their accounts of this event, nor did they want our interpretations to focus on damage control. Surely they wrote of this event because they believed it could enrich our understanding of Jesus. And indeed, if we refuse to uncritically accept the violent version that's often taught, we'll come to see that this event actually advances our understanding of how Jesus makes peace.

The Gospels divide Jesus' temple cleansing into three phases—the preparation, action, and explanation. Each phase has a valuable lesson to teach us about Jesus' approach to peacemaking.

PHASE 1: PREPARATION

The previous chapter ended with Jesus still en route to Jerusalem. With so many people celebrating his arrival, one might expect some sort of climactic conclusion to the day's events. It didn't happen. The gospel of Mark simply states, "Jesus entered Jerusalem and went into the temple courts. He looked around at everything, but since it was already late, he went out to Bethany with the Twelve" (11:11).

At first glance, it appears that nothing important occurred during Jesus' brief visit to the temple Sunday evening. He merely looked around and then left. That's it. Nevertheless, though it may seem insignificant, the simple act of *looking around* was actually a crucial step in Jesus' approach to peacemaking. As Ched Myers notes, "Jesus' initial visit to the temple [was] for reconnaissance."[6] What he saw bothered him. Something was terribly wrong, and he was not going to let it go unchallenged.

Yet instead of responding impulsively then and there, Jesus waited until the next day to act, thus giving himself time to devise a plan. When he returned to the temple on Monday, his conduct was not rash or impetuous—in contrast to how it is often portrayed. Rather, as with his triumphal entry the day before, Jesus' actions were purposeful and deliberate, calculated and planned.

Lesson 1: Christlike peacemakers assess before they act.

Jesus' reconnaissance mission demonstrates the importance of assessing situations before jumping into action. This may sound obvious, yet history is replete with examples of well-meaning people entering into places of need and immediately enacting their predetermined plans. Such ill-informed attempts at cultivating peace usually cause more harm than good.

While living in Vancouver's Downtown Eastside, I often encountered out-of-town church groups performing drive-by-feedings. The whole streamlined operation usually went something like this: A large van pulls over and fifteen smiling faces emerge. Someone yells, "Free food!" as a line of people not-so-miraculously materializes. Then, while one church member strums a guitar and belts praise songs, the rest of the group hands out bagged meals. Minutes later, when the food runs out, the group hops back in their van and drives off into the sunset.

After witnessing more than one of these "rapid acts of kindness," I saw a familiar pattern emerge. Once the church van left, arguments inevitably broke out between those who received a meal and those who did not.

What's more, my neighbors didn't actually need free food. Soon after moving to the area, my friend Craig Greenfield and I spent a week voluntarily homeless on the streets of the Downtown Eastside. We wanted to assess the situation, learn directly from our neighbors experiencing homelessness, and see what challenges they faced. That week, we discovered you could get free meals twenty-three times a day in the Downtown Eastside. Nobody was starving for food. Of course, none of those well-intentioned outsiders knew this, since they devised a plan without first *assessing* the situation.

PHASE 2: ACTION

When Jesus returned to the temple on Monday, he entered the Court of the Gentiles to implement his plan. All four gospels describe Jesus' actions, and their accounts share many similarities. For example, Matthew, Mark, and Luke each speak of Jesus sending out the sellers.[7] And all but Luke mention Jesus flipping over the tables of the money changers. But there is one crucial detail found only in John's account of this event. He alone states that Jesus used a whip.

This mention of a whip has led many to conclude that Jesus acted violently. Such a conclusion, however, rests on the assumption that Jesus whipped people. But what does the gospel of John actually say about Jesus' use of a whip? Did Jesus whip people? Given the tragic history of Jesus' whip being co-opted as pretext for violence, this question deserves careful consideration. So at this point in the chapter, we're going to slow down, take our time, and carefully examine each piece of evidence, beginning with what John wrote about the whip itself.

Evidence #1: The whip

According to the gospel of John, upon entering the temple court, Jesus "made a whip out of cords" (2:15). Notice that John explicitly states that Jesus made the whip once he was already in the temple. John also specifically names cords as the material Jesus used to construct his whip. The Greek word *schoinion*, which the NIV translates generically as "cords," more precisely refers to "rushes or reeds, akin to rattan or wicker material."[8]

Years ago, I sought to see if such a whip could actually cause bodily harm. So I bought two hundred feet of wicker material and tried to make the most intimidating whip possible. I worked hard, took my time, and tried multiple designs. But in the end, despite hours of effort, my wicker-whip creations never could have injured anyone. If Jesus had wildly waved a whip like mine at people, they would have fallen over laughing instead of fleeing in fear. The best that could be said about my prototypes is that they roughly resembled a whip.

Interestingly, John appears to say the same about Jesus' whip. The two oldest manuscripts we have of the gospel of John, the Bodmer papyri $\mathfrak{P}^{66}$ and $\mathfrak{P}^{75}$, both include the little Greek word *hōs* before the word for whip.[9] The word *hōs* means to approximate something. In Luke 22:44, for example, *hōs* is used to state that Jesus sweat *something like* blood while praying on the Mount of Olives. So if *hōs* was originally included in John's account of the temple cleansing—which is what our earliest textual witnesses indicate—then the passage actually reads that Jesus "made *something like* a whip out of cords."

If Jesus' pseudo-whip was anything like my wicker-whip creations, then it's hard to imagine how one man could drive all the sellers and money changers out of the temple with such a primitive "weapon."

Either way, here's what we know for sure about the whip: John's gospel does not describe a well-designed instrument of torture. It was not constructed by a skilled craftsperson under ideal conditions with choice materials and plenty of time. Rather, it was a makeshift whip that Jesus assembled hastily from a limited selection of available materials.

Evidence #2: The sheep and cattle

In fact, this raises the question, Where within the Court of the Gentiles did Jesus find this wicker-like material? The prevailing theory—first proposed by Catholic scholar Raymond Brown—is that Jesus "fashioned his whip from the rushes used as bedding for the animals."[10] Since we have detailed records of the items typically found in the temple, it's hard to explain where else Jesus might have acquired this sort of material.

If Jesus used animal bedding to construct his whip, which is our best guess, then it means that Jesus was already near the sheep and cattle (John 2:14–15). What's more, primitive whips, like the one Jesus made, are known to have been used in antiquity to herd such animals.[11] That is to say, the sheep and cattle likely recognized this type of herding implement. By repeatedly striking the ground with his whip, Jesus could have easily shooed these animals away.

Moreover, there was no need for Jesus to forcefully remove the animal sellers. To get them out of the temple, all Jesus needed to do was cause their source of income to flee the scene. By driving the sheep and cattle out of the temple, the sellers would have hightailed it after their livelihood, thus killing two birds with one stone—figuratively speaking, of course.

Evidence #3: Temple security

If Jesus hurt anyone in the temple, then it is difficult to explain why security personnel did not intervene. The temple employed armed guards, and an entire garrison of Roman soldiers kept watch over the temple from the adjacent tower of Fortress Antonia. Their primary task was to intervene if unrest ever erupted in the temple. Such a disturbance occurred in Acts 21, for example, when the temple crowd tried to kill Paul. In that instance, Roman soldiers quickly stepped in and put a stop to the crowd's violent intentions (Acts 21:27–36).

If Jesus became violent, then Rome's lack of response is all the more surprising given the timing of this event. As we saw previously, Rome was particularly sensitive to the risk of revolt during the volatile Passover festivities. This concern led Pilate to assign additional troops to help surveil the temple from the tower of Antonia. As Jesus moved about the temple on the second day of Passover, scores of soldiers would have been watching him, ready to pounce at the first sign of rabble-rousing.

After all, here was a fringe religious leader whose charismatic ministry had amassed a huge Jewish following. If any had doubted the extent of his popularity, yesterday's procession proved it was both large and impassioned. For one man to have this much influence over the masses was dangerous. Undoubtedly, the Romans were keeping a close eye on Jesus. Their lack of a response, therefore, suggests that Rome did not view Jesus' actions as a threat.

Evidence #4: The Greek of John 2:15

The whip, the animals, and the temple security all favor a nonviolent interpretation of Jesus' temple cleansing. Yet they hold little weight if John's account explicitly states in the original Greek text that Jesus whipped people. To answer our question with any degree of certainty, we must look at what John actually wrote about Jesus' use of the whip.

The crucial sentence is found in John 2:15. According to the NKJV, it reads, "When He had made a whip of cords, He drove them all out of the temple, with the sheep and the oxen." This suggests that Jesus whipped both people and animals. But other translations, like the NRSV and NIV, understand Jesus to have whipped only the sheep and cattle. The NIV, for example, states: "So he made a whip out of cords, and drove all from the temple courts, both sheep and cattle." So which is it? What does the Greek text actually say?

If we translate the Greek literally, without smoothing it out in English, the sentence begins, "He drove out from the temple *all*." If John had stopped the sentence at this point, there would be no way to know whether Jesus whipped people or whether he whipped animals. Grammatically speaking, the *all* in this verse can refer to either the animal sellers and money changers *or* the sheep and cattle. Either interpretation is equally valid.

Thankfully, however, John did not end the verse with the word *all*. Knowing the ambiguity this would cause, John continued the sentence by adding a clarifying phrase: "And making a whip out of cords, he drove out from the temple all, *te* the sheep *kai* the cattle."

Our quest to determine whether Jesus whipped people or animals ultimately rests on how we translate phrases that utilize this "*te* [noun] *kai* [noun]" construction. Fortunately, these constructions are quite common. They occur ninety-one times in the New Testament—once here in John 2:15 and ninety times elsewhere.

Here's the staggering reality: Every other time in the New Testament when a "*te* [noun] *kai* [noun]" phrase is used to modify a noun (as it does in John 2:15), it is clearly being used to tell us what that noun consists of.[12] Explained differently, it lists the parts that make up the whole. Consider two examples:

Luke 22:66	"the council of the elders of the people, both [*te*] the chief priests and [*kai*] the teachers of the law"
1 Corinthians 1:24	"those whom God has called, both [*te*] Jews and [*kai*] Greeks"

In both examples, the "*te* [noun] *kai* [noun]" phrase breaks down the noun it modifies into its constituent parts. "The council," we learn, was made up of "both the chief priests and the teachers of the law." And "those whom God has called" consisted of "both Jews and Greeks."

Now, wouldn't it be great if there were other instances of a "*te* [noun] *kai* [noun]" phrase modifying the word *all*, just as it does in John 2:15? Such close grammatical parallels would surely inform how we ought to translate John 2:15. Thankfully, this happens eleven other times in the New Testament. In each case, the "*te* [noun] *kai* [noun]" phrase clearly tells us what the *all* is comprised of. A few examples will suffice (the full list of occurrences can be found in the notes[13]):

Matthew 22:10 NRSV	"*all* whom they found, both [*te*] good and [*kai*] bad"
Acts 19:10 NRSV	"*all* the residents of Asia, both [*te*] Jews and [*kai*] Greeks"
Romans 3:9 NRSV	"we have already charged that *all*, both [*te*] Jews and [*kai*] Greeks, are under the power of sin"
Revelation 19:18 NRSV	"[the] flesh of *all*, both [*te*] free and [*kai*] slave"

Each of the other seven occasions where a "*te* [noun] *kai* [noun]" phrase modifies the word *all* is translated in kind—*all, both x and y.*

The astonishing consistency of this phrase's canonical usage leads New Testament scholar N. Clayton Croy to conclude, "It is very difficult to construe the Greek [of John 2:15] as meaning anything but "both the sheep and the oxen."[14] Stating the case more forcefully, theologian Brooke Foss Westcott concludes, "[The] clause must be translated, *both the sheep and the oxen.*"[15]

When John added a "*te* [noun] *kai* [noun]" phrase to the end of this verse, he did so to specify what Jesus drove out of the temple with a whip. The *all* of this verse consisted of both sheep and cattle. "And making a whip out of cords, he drove out from the temple all, both sheep and cattle" (2:15). "This translation," theological ethicist Andy Alexis-Baker notes, "puts John 2:15 in line with how translators universally translate all of the other 90 uses of *te . . . kai* in the New Testament."[16] In other words, to claim that Jesus whipped people, one must translate the "*te* [noun] *kai* [noun]" phrase of John 2:15 in a way it's never used elsewhere.

A consistent witness of nonviolence

This conclusion—that John does not describe Jesus whipping people—should come as no surprise. If Jesus had whipped the money changers and animal sellers, then it would be the only instance in the Gospels of him using violence. It would have contradicted Jesus' clear teaching about the impermissibility of violence (e.g., Matthew 5:39, 44). And it would have refuted Isaiah's insistence that God's future messiah would be killed despite "[having] done no violence" (53:9).

In fact, when on trial later in the week, Jesus would highlight his innocence by appealing to his peaceful activities in the temple. Not even the false witnesses at Jesus' trial would accuse him of violence. In their efforts to entrap Jesus, surely they would not have withheld such damning evidence if it existed.

Put simply, there is zero credible evidence to support a violent interpretation of Jesus cleansing the temple.

Lesson 2: Christlike peacemakers are not passive.

Though Jesus whipped no people, one could argue that his actions still contradict his peace teaching. After all, while he may not have hurt anyone, Jesus still appears to have been angry, assertive, and aggressive. He was still flipping over tables, pouring out coins, and giving the dove sellers a good tongue-lashing. Even if such actions are not violent, how do they square with Jesus' approach to peacemaking? Perhaps the following scenario will help us gain a new perspective on Jesus' actions:

> One day a mother gets off work early. So she drives home, opens the front door, and walks into the living room, where—much to her horror—she discovers that her teenage son and his friends are high on prescription painkillers. Instantly, the mother snaps into action. She grabs the pill bottle and flips over the coffee table it had been on. Then she rushes into the bathroom, pours the painkillers into the toilet, and flushes them down the drain. Finally, the mom returns to the living room, looks the boys in the eye, and while choking back tears says, "Your bodies are made in the image of God. Stop destroying them with drugs."

Now let me ask you: Was this mother angry, assertive, and aggressive? I suppose you could view her actions that way. Did she flip over a table, pour out the drugs, and give a firm lecture to the teens? You bet she did. And that is exactly what any caring parent would do. In fact, we would accuse this mother of negligence if she hadn't intervened. Clearly, her actions were motivated by love, by a deep desire to see these boys no longer destroy their lives.

What if Jesus' actions were motivated by the same kind of love? Was Jesus angry, assertive, and aggressive? I suppose you could view his actions that way. Did Jesus flip over tables, pour out coins, and give a firm lecture to the animal sellers and money changers? You bet he did. And that is exactly what our caring God does. Like a loving mother snapping into action, God intervenes to make things right.

Our understanding of how Jesus makes peace is advanced, not undermined, by his actions in the temple. The gospel accounts of this event reveal that Jesus was not violent, but neither was he passive. In the temple cleansing, we discover the one whom Gandhi called "the most active resister known to history."[17]

For Jesus, pacifism could never be equated with passivism. Refusing to act violently was never a refusal to act. When all was not right, Jesus never sat idly by, doing nothing. Love compelled him to act. Love moved him to resist evil with every fiber of his being. And Jesus intends for this same active love to be found in all who embrace his approach to peacemaking.

PHASE 3: EXPLANATION

Already in this chapter, we've gleaned two valuable lessons in peacemaking. We've covered a lot of ground, yet if we stopped here, Jesus' actions would be stripped from their context. If we want to be a people who care about the same things Jesus cared about, then we still need to identify the issue or issues that upset him.

Thankfully, we don't have to speculate about what provoked Jesus. After disrupting the temple's operations, Jesus—in keeping with prophetic tradition—explained his actions. To do so, he quoted two well-known lines from the Hebrew prophets Isaiah and Jeremiah: "As [Jesus] taught them, he said, 'Is it not written: "My house will be called a house of prayer for all nations"? But you have made it "a den of robbers"'" (Mark 11:17).

Isaiah's vision of radical inclusion

The first reference—"My house will be called a house of prayer for all nations"—is a direct quote from Isaiah 56:7. To explain his temple action, Jesus began by aligning himself with one of the most radical visions in the Hebrew Scriptures of God's all-inclusive love.

According to Isaiah's vision, the temple was intended to be a place that embodied God's gracious inclusivity. In the temple, foreigners were to be welcomed (56:3, 6–7) and outsiders taken in (v. 4–5). In God's house, those normally excluded by society were to be given "a name better than sons and daughters" (v. 5). In short, God's temple was to serve as "a house of prayer for all nations" (v. 7).

Moreover, God did not just declare an open invitation and then sit back and wait to see who would respond. According to Isaiah, God was actively gathering the excluded into the temple (v. 8), and God expected the temple priests to help make this divine prerogative a reality.

But instead of the temple shining as a beacon of lavish welcome, Jesus found it promoting an ideology of segregation. The temple's original design did not include a separate court for foreigners. This "court of the excluded" was added, missiologist Scott Bessenecker explains, because devout Jewish men had grown increasingly sensitive to purity laws.[18] Once the court was built, foreigners were confined within, and numerous signs warned them that venturing beyond would result in death.

Adding insult to injury, temple merchants set up shop during Passover in the only part of the temple open to foreigners. Overrun with noisy animals, bulky tables, and lengthy lines, foreigners would have found their worship greatly disrupted. As New Testament scholar Andreas Köstenberger observes, the decision to convert the Court of the Gentiles into an open-air market was "insensitive at best and evidence of religious arrogance at worst."[19]

Jeremiah's charge against exploitation

After quoting from Isaiah 56, Jesus then cited Jeremiah's lament that the temple had become "a den of robbers" (Jeremiah

7:11). Centuries earlier, Jeremiah had stood in the temple and warned God's people to stop behaving as if their participation in temple activities excused their unjust lifestyles.

According to Jeremiah, God wanted his people to "deal with each other justly" (v. 5). But instead, they were oppressing foreigners, orphans, and widows (v. 6). They were stealing, murdering, lying, and committing idolatry (v. 9). To make matters worse, Jeremiah's listeners behaved as if the offering of sacrifices won them God's favor. They assumed, as many do today, that worship in God's house covers over a multitude of sins.

Thus, God spoke through Jeremiah, warning, "Do not trust in deceptive words and say, 'This is the temple of the LORD, the temple of the LORD, the temple of the LORD!'" (v. 4). And do not "come and stand before me in this house, which bears my Name, and say, 'We are safe'—safe to do all these detestable things" (v. 10).

All of this led Jeremiah to liken the temple to a "den of robbers" (v. 11). It is a fitting image, for, as Marcus Borg and John Dominic Crossan write, "The people's everyday injustice makes them robbers, and they think the temple is their safe house, den, hideaway, or place of security."[20]

Much like Jeremiah, when Jesus looked around the temple he saw an institution corrupted by greed. Not only were its leaders raking in huge profits as they exploited the religious devotion of the masses, but the very heart of temple worship had been commercialized.

The whole sacrificial system rested on the purchasing of animals. And since these purchases could be paid for only with Tyrian shekels, money changers were needed to convert the more commonly used Roman coinage. Because the animal sellers and money changers controlled two essential services, they were able to charge exorbitant prices that threatened to exclude the poorest members of society from participating in temple worship.

The money changers, for instance, not only charged sky-high currency exchange rates but also added a hefty surcharge to each transaction. According to the Mishnah, which is a written compilation of Jewish oral traditions codified at the end of the second century, the surcharge that the money changers added to the temple tax brought in enough profit to pay for all the gold plating used to cover the entire holy of holies.[21]

There is also a fascinating historical account of price gouging by the animal sellers. A few decades after Jesus' temple incident, a prominent member of the Sanhedrin, Simeon, son of Gamaliel I, learned that a pair of doves were being sold for two gold dinars. Doves were the staple animal purchased by the poor for sacrifices, and Simeon feared this inflated price would prevent many from participating in worship. So Simeon stood in the temple court, publicly chastised the dove sellers, and vowed to not rest until a pair of doves could be bought for one silver dinar. That same day, the price plummeted a whopping 99 percent.[22]

As wealth poured into the temple, much of it ultimately lined the pockets of the high priestly families. Those who held this position lived in great luxury. Both Annas and Caiaphas, for example, resided in large homes within the walls of Jerusalem and employed multiple domestic servants. And decades later, the historian Josephus dubbed the high priest Ananias the "great procurer of money."[23]

Cleaning house

Jesus used the words of Isaiah and Jeremiah to explain that his actions sought to stop the temple's exploitative and marginalizing practices. By overturning tables and driving out animals, Jesus suspended the temple's commercial operations. Profiteering came to a halt. And by sending away the perpetrators of injustice, Jesus made room for the excluded to be welcomed in.

When discussing the temple cleansing, we often overlook the fact that after the money changers and animal sellers went out, the blind and lame came in and were healed (Matthew 21:14). For these marginalized people, their admittance into the temple was just as miraculous as the physical healing they received. Mosaic law prohibited those with physical defects from offering sacrifices (Leviticus 21:16–24), and David had banned them from ever entering the temple (2 Samuel 5:8). Matthew goes on to write that children also entered the temple courts and praised Jesus (21:15). Their presence in the temple is equally astonishing, for, as theologian Stanley Hauerwas notes, "children had always been excluded from the temple."[24]

Jesus' explanation also reveals that he was particularly concerned about evil done in God's name. There were obviously numerous institutions in antiquity that marginalized outsiders and exploited the poor. Yet of them all, Jesus focused his condemnation on the temple. Why single out this religious institution?

Perhaps Jesus targeted the temple because, as the place where God was said to dwell, people believed that what happened there reflected the heart of God. When religion legitimizes injustice, it communicates to the world that God wills such evil. It makes God appear wicked. By marginalizing foreigners, the temple made God look like a tribal deity who was only concerned with the well-being of God's own people. And by economically exploiting the poor, the temple portrayed

God as yet another greedy ruler with an insatiable hunger for his subjects' hard-earned money.

On Holy Monday, Jesus refused to let this corrupt portrayal of God go unchallenged. He was zealous for people to know that God is good. Thus, on one of the temple's busiest days of the year, Jesus entered the temple and publicly challenged its distorted projection of God. What's more, Jesus even proclaimed that *he*, not the temple, was "the real meeting place between God and man."[25] In him, heaven and earth meet. In him, we discover what God is truly like.

Lesson 3: Instead of injuring and destroying, Christlike peacemakers channel their zeal into acts that heal and restore.

On the second day of Holy Week, Jesus zealously confronted injustice and defended God's goodness. As we seek to cultivate peace, we must also passionately address such issues. But as students of Christ's approach to peacemaking, we face the added challenge of ensuring that our zeal is not misguided.

In the last chapter, we saw how zeal for God led Mattathias to kill a fellow Jew who was about to offer a sacrifice to pagan gods. His son Judas Maccabeus was equally zealous to serve God, so he picked up the sword of the revolutionary and slaughtered those he perceived to be God's enemies. And now, on Holy Monday, we find the chief priests so zealous to maintain their control of God's house that in response to Jesus' temple stunt, they "began looking for a way to kill him" (Mark 11:18).

Jesus was also zealous to serve God. Yet instead of Jesus injuring or killing others in a violent rage, his zeal resulted in the healing and inclusion of those who had been excluded from the temple. Such fervor also came at great personal cost. As Jesus cleansed the temple, his disciples remembered that it was written of him: "Zeal for your house will consume me" (John 2:17). The Greek verb translated here as "consume" means "to eat up, devour, or utterly destroy." In other words, in his zeal for God, Jesus refused to consume others, though he was willing to be consumed.

"This is the fundamental transformation that Jesus brought to the theme of zeal," writes Pope Benedict XVI in his book on Holy Week. "The 'zeal' that would serve God through violence he transformed into . . . the zeal of self-giving love."[26]

Many claim their zeal is righteous. But don't be fooled. On Monday of Holy Week, Jesus revealed what true zeal for God looks like. Truly righteous zeal is constructive, not destructive. It lifts others up instead of tearing them down. Instead of injuring, it heals. Instead of destroying, it restores. And above all, truly righteous zeal is motivated by self-giving love, not other-consuming hatred.

THE SEQUEL

It took great courage for Jesus to confront the temple authorities with this sort of zeal. Only the bravest would dare such a feat. After all, speaking truth to power is risky business. It can get you killed. So who in their right mind would risk rolling the dice a second time? Who would chance another encounter?

I'll give you one guess.

Tomorrow, Jesus will return to the temple. Only this time, instead of confronting the temple authorities, they will confront him.

4

Tuesday

Traps, Truth-Telling, and Traitors

Even if you're a Bible-reading, Sunday school–attending, church-loving Christian who can name Jacob's twelve sons in alphabetical order and rattle off obscure Bible trivia, chances are you can't recall a single thing that happened on Tuesday of Holy Week. Why is that?

It's not because the Gospels skip over this day. In fact, no other day receives more attention in the Gospels than Tuesday of Holy Week. Matthew, for example, has more to say about this day than all the other days of Holy Week combined. Even his coverage of the Sermon on the Mount—which spans three whole chapters—is only half as long.

So why can't we remember anything that happened on the most talked-about day of the most important week in Jesus' life? Perhaps it's because Tuesday's content is largely dialogue-based, while other days of Holy Week contain riveting scenes that grab our attention. From the waving of palms to the scattering of alms, from a traitorous kiss to nail-pierced wrists, it's hard for Tuesday to compete with such memorable moments.

Yet I think there is a deeper, less benign reason for overlooking Holy Tuesday. Simply put, we've been trained to do so. Not intentionally, of course. Nevertheless, it has been done habitually. Though our churches never explicitly say to ignore Holy Tuesday, most have encouraged such behavior by the way they commemorate the week. Year after year, when Holy Week rolls around, most churches celebrate Palm Sunday and then do nothing else until Thursday evening arrives. As a result, the events of Monday, Tuesday, and Wednesday get brushed aside as incidental.

It seems we are in a hurry to get to the cross. And while that's understandable—for it's tempting to skip the lead-up when you can go straight to the main event—doing so comes at a cost. In our passion to lift up the cross, we've accidentally uprooted it from its context and severed it from the life of the One who gives it meaning. Ironically, our attempts to make much of the cross have actually diminished its significance.

Unlike us, the gospel writers did not rush past the first half of Holy Week. They took their time detailing the days leading up to the cross. And when it came to Holy Tuesday, they decided numerous developments were worth chronicling. In fact, given how much they wrote, one could argue that they considered Holy Tuesday to be of the utmost importance.

The day begins with Jesus returning to the temple. At first glance, his decision to go back to the site of yesterday's altercation seems a death wish. After all, because of Monday's stunt, the chief priests and teachers of the law were now "looking for a way to kill him" (Mark 11:18). His whip-wielding antics had threatened their status as the official overseers of Jewish religious life. Such an assault on their authority could not go unchallenged. Jesus must be disposed of.

Knowing their intentions, why would Jesus voluntarily return to the lair of those seeking to devour him?

Although the move appears suicidal, the temple may have actually been the only safe place left for Jesus. That's because the site teemed with his supporters. The crowds that gathered in the temple's large open-air courtyard were on Jesus' side. And if anything, his actions on the previous day—which temporarily decommercialized the temple—only served to strengthen their approval of him.

Matthew writes that the temple authorities "looked for a way to arrest [Jesus], but they were afraid of the crowd" (21:46). How infuriating it must have been for their hands to be tied when Jesus stood but an arm's length away. As long as Jesus had the approval of the masses, the religious leaders could not touch him. Somehow, they needed to convince Jesus' admirers to turn on him. One way or another, they needed to discredit Jesus while all were watching. With that goal in mind, it wasn't long before the chief priests, teachers of the law, and elders hatched a plan.

Thus, the stage was set and the characters were in position for the great drama of Holy Tuesday to begin. The Gospels divide the day into three separate acts. In the first, the temple authorities ask Jesus a series of baited questions in hopes that his supporters will turn on him when he inevitably misspeaks. Much to their amazement, however, Jesus evades each trap. After emerging victorious, Jesus goes on the offensive in the day's second act. He launches into a lengthy critique of the religious leaders that culminates in a series of warnings. And finally, in the last act, after exiting the temple, the disciples ask Jesus when a prediction he made will come to pass. His answer unsettles them.

Because Tuesday's content is so extensive, this chapter will focus on just three texts, one from each section of the day. Rather than cherry-pick the passages that best advance our understanding of peacemaking, I've chosen the ones that seem to most undermine it. Each passage has a history of being misused by Christians to justify violence. But the time has come to reclaim these texts for what they truly are: exemplars of peacemaking. If it can be shown that Jesus was contending for peace even in these instances, then the flag of peace will have been firmly planted in Tuesday's hallowed ground.

We begin with the second baited question that the religious leaders asked Jesus:

RENDER UNTO CAESAR

> Later they sent some of the Pharisees and Herodians to Jesus to catch him in his words. They came to him and said, "Teacher, we know that you are a man of integrity. You aren't swayed by others, because you pay no attention to who they are; but you teach the way of God in accordance with the truth. Is it right to pay the imperial tax to Caesar or not? Should we pay or shouldn't we?"
>
> But Jesus knew their hypocrisy. "Why are you trying to trap me?" he asked. "Bring me a denarius and let me look at it." They brought the coin, and he asked them, "Whose image is this? And whose inscription?"
>
> "Caesar's," they replied.
>
> Then Jesus said to them, "Give back to Caesar what is Caesar's and to God what is God's."
>
> And they were amazed at him.
>
> —Mark 12:13–17

Nobody likes paying taxes. But for the people of Judea, taxation was more than just a hefty economic burden. It also signified their lack of autonomy. They were not free. They were subjects of Rome. And the empire's mandatory poll tax reminded them of this every year.

The tax was first imposed on the people of Judea when their province came under direct Roman rule in AD 6. Since every adult Jew was required to pay, Rome ordered that a census be taken to calculate how much the region would owe. The census and resulting taxation were fiercely opposed by Jewish nationalists. In fact, at the time, a Galilean named Judas—perhaps inspired by his Maccabean namesake—led a popular tax revolt. Even though many joined his cause, in the end Judas's anti-tax movement proved no match to the power of Rome. The revolt was quickly crushed, and according to Acts 5:37, Judas was executed.

Now, decades later, another popular Galilean stood before the chief priests, teachers of the law, and elders. This second Galilean bore many similarities to his predecessor. In fact, Jesus had even adopted Judas's motto.[1] The motto spoke, as theologian and Nazi resister Dietrich Bonhoeffer would later write, of the need to rally around one all-encompassing allegiance. It stated in no uncertain terms that there could be only one true leader. All other lords and loyalties were rejected. It's a motto that still gets used to this day. One that you've likely repeated many times: the kingdom of God.

As Marcus Borg and John Dominic Crossan note, "Jesus could have spoken of the family of God, the community of God, or the people of God," but instead, he chose a politically loaded slogan.[2] And now the religious leaders were ready to trap him with a question that was equally political in nature.

The spokesmen

In order for their plan to succeed, however, the chief priests, teachers of the law, and elders needed to first overcome one major obstacle. For although they had crafted the perfect question, one that was guaranteed to catch Jesus in his words, they could not actually ask Jesus their question. If they had inquired of Jesus themselves, everyone would have known their question was a sham. Why? Because they were in charge of collecting the unpopular tax.

Thus, the gospel of Mark tells us that in their stead "they sent some of the Pharisees and Herodians" to inquire of Jesus (12:13). It was a brilliant move, since these two groups genuinely disagreed on whether the tax should be paid. The Herodians were lackeys of the Roman government and generally approved of the poll tax. The Pharisees, on the other hand, resisted Roman intrusion and despised the tax.[3] By sending spokesmen from these two groups, the question was made to appear sincere. The real motive behind the inquiry—to trap Jesus—was concealed and could ultimately be denied.

The setup

Even the best-laid trap is destined to fail unless you find a way to lure your prey to it. That is why, before launching into their actual question, the Herodians and Pharisees first tried to draw Jesus in with some cunning flattery:

"Teacher, we know that you are a man of integrity. You aren't swayed by others, because you pay no attention to who they are; but you teach the way of God in accordance with the truth" (Mark 12:14).

In essence, as theologian Ched Myers notes, the Herodians and Pharisees praised Jesus for always "telling the truth regardless of the consequences."[4] They commended him for not being swayed by public opinion. Far from innocent, their opening cajolery dared Jesus to take a public stand on the divisive issue they were about to raise, even if doing so resulted in his downfall.

The trap

After luring Jesus in with praise, the Herodians and Pharisees set their trap. "Is it right to pay the imperial tax to Caesar or not?" they asked. "Should we pay or shouldn't we?" (Mark 12:14–15). The question was purposefully designed to allow only two possible answers: yes or no, pay or don't pay.

If Jesus answered yes, pay the tax, he'd immediately discredit himself before the crowds who both loathed the tax and expected Jesus to rid them of the Romans. If he answered no, don't pay the tax, the authorities could arrest him for inciting revolt. In other words, either response would be his undoing.

Thus, the trap was set. Jesus was cornered. And this time, it looked like the religious leaders would finally catch their prey.

The escape

The thing about traps, however, is that they're indiscriminate in what they catch. Whether you're the hunter or the hunted, if you step in one, it will snap shut.

> "Why are you trying to trap me?" [Jesus] asked. "Bring me a denarius and let me look at it." They brought the coin, and he asked them, "Whose image is this? And whose inscription?"
> "Caesar's," they replied. (Mark 12:15–16)

With lightning speed, over the course of this brief exchange Jesus masterfully evaded capture and tricked his questioners into entrapping themselves. But in order to see how he did this, you need to know a few things about the coinage used to pay Rome's poll tax.

The denarius was the standard silver coin minted by Rome. On the front was the face of Tiberius Caesar, encircled with the words "Tiberius Caesar, Son of the Divine Augustus." The reverse side displayed an image of the goddess of peace. The coin was pure propaganda, and as theologian and New Testament scholar N. T. Wright explains, its message was clear: "Look at the face, pay the tax, and the son of God, the true high priest, will give you peace."[5]

Understandably, pious Jews refused to carry this coin since its inscription and portraits violated the first and second commandments. God's people were not to worship any other gods or to possess any graven images. Knowing this, Rome permitted the Jews to produce their own non-idolatrous coins, with which the poll tax could be paid.[6] The empire didn't care *how* the tax was paid so long as it *was* paid.

Thus, by asking to see a denarius, Jesus revealed that he did not possess such a coin. But in handing him one, the Herodians and Pharisees unwittingly disclosed before a watching crowd that they did. Even worse, as R. T. France notes in his commentary on Matthew's gospel, they had brought the idolatrous coin into the holy precincts of the temple![7]

Before the significance of what just happened could sink in, Jesus made his next move. With the denarius now in his hand, Jesus looked at it and noticed someone's face imprinted on it. So he asked, "Whose image is this?" As if the answer was obvious, the Herodians and Pharisees promptly replied, "Caesar's" (Mark 12:16).

In that moment, his questioners' opening flattery—which they thought was so cunning—came back to bite them. "You aren't swayed by others," they had said of Jesus, "because you pay no attention to who they are" (Mark 12:14). As Wright points out, the latter phrase is the NIV's attempt to convey in English the essential meaning of a Jewish idiom that literally reads in Greek, "You don't look at people's faces."[8] Thus, by asking whose image was on the coin, Jesus confirmed that he did not look to the face of Caesar for protection and peace. But evidently, as their swift reply suggests, the Herodians and Pharisees did.

Check and mate! "Even before the famous words about rendering to Caesar," write Borg and Crossan, "Jesus has won the encounter."[9]

The answer

A prudent man would have stopped at this point. After all, Jesus had nothing to gain and everything to lose if he continued. But evidently, Jesus believed their trap presented a unique teaching opportunity, for upon being told that the coin's image belonged to Caesar, Jesus uttered his now famous answer, "Give back to Caesar what is Caesar's and to God what is God's" (Mark 12:17a). The scene then quickly ends with the recognition that all were *amazed* at Jesus' answer (v. 17b).

Apparently, the crowd heard something profound in Jesus' reply. Something that took them aback and left them in awe. In fact, the Greek verb that Mark chose to use, *ekthaumazō*, denotes being amazed to a high degree. In other words, the crowd was more than just slightly intrigued by Jesus' answer. They *marveled greatly* at the brilliance of his words. Its profundity left them *utterly astonished*.

We, on the other hand, tend to think Jesus' answer is downright commonsensical, as if he was merely stating the obvious, that which we all already know to be true. "Of course, we must give to God and country what each are due," we tell ourselves. "That's what's required of you when you're a citizen of both a heavenly kingdom and an earthly nation."

Yet this cannot be what Jesus meant by his answer, for if it was, the crowd would have responded with anger, not amazement. Anyone who claimed—especially on religious grounds—that Caesar's tax should be paid was a traitor to the Jewish cause. The only credible explanation for the crowd's reaction is that they interpreted Jesus' words differently than we do. And here, I believe, is why they did: Because Jesus and his listeners were all Jews, they read the same sacred texts in the same shared language. Thus, when Jesus replaced two of his questioners' key words with biblically important alternatives, those listening in the temple knew exactly what he meant.

Faces versus images

In their opening remarks, as we've already discussed, the Herodians and Pharisees praised Jesus for not looking at people's *faces*. But instead of repeating their word in his reply, Jesus asked whose *image* was on the coin. This subtle change in words may seem insignificant. But once Jesus gave his final answer, it appears that the crowd quickly connected the dots. They realized Jesus was alluding to the central Jewish tenet that all of humanity is created in God's *image*. The implication is this: Since the coin has Caesar's *image* imprinted on it, give it back to him. Let him keep his idolatrous money. But as Andreas Köstenberger and Justin Taylor observe, since we have God's *image* imprinted on us, "we owe everything—all that we have and all that we are—to him."[10]

Paying versus repaying

The second word that Jesus replaced reinforces this interpretation. Back when they posed their question, the Herodians and Pharisees asked whether it was right *to pay* the imperial tax. But in his answer, Jesus reframed the question by using a markedly different word, the verb *apodidōmi*, which means to repay, give back, or return. The brilliance of this word swap lies in the fact that before you can *return* something to someone, you first need to know to whom it belongs. You can't give back to Caesar what is Caesar's, for instance, without first identifying what is rightfully his to begin with. Thus, by switching verbs, Jesus revealed that the answer to their tax question lies in answering an even deeper set of questions; namely: What belongs to Caesar? And what belongs to God?

Any Jew with even a cursory understanding of the Scriptures would have immediately known the answer to the second question: Everything belongs to God. Everything. It's a refrain that runs throughout the Old Testament. "The earth is the LORD's, and everything in it, the world, and all who live in it," declared the psalmist (24:1). The author of 1 Chronicles adds, "Everything in heaven and earth is yours. Yours, LORD, is the kingdom. . . . You are the ruler of all things. . . . Everything comes from you, and we have given you only what comes from your hand" (29:11–14).[11]

But if everything belongs to God, what's left for Caesar? What do we owe the Caesars of this world? The logical answer seems to be *nothing*. Indeed, that's what the religious leaders understood Jesus to be saying, for later in the week, they will drag Jesus before Pontius Pilate and accuse him of "oppos[ing] payment of taxes to Caesar" (Luke 23:2).

The apostles and earliest Christians, however, gave a more nuanced answer to the question, "What belongs to Caesar?" They taught that since everything belongs to God, we owe Caesar only those things that align with God's will. So, for instance, when ordered to no longer preach about Jesus, the apostles refused to comply, stating, "We must obey God rather than human beings!" (Acts 5:29). Caesar's demands were valid only if they did not conflict with God's will.

A rending of the render

Beginning in the mid-second century, however, a new way of interpreting Jesus' tax answer emerged, one that has persuaded countless Christians to fight on Caesar's behalf.[12] About AD 154, Justin Martyr wrote a defense of Christianity that he hoped would convince Emperor Antonius Pius to stop persecuting Christians. In it, Justin quotes Jesus' "render unto Caesar" saying and then offers the following interpretation: "Whence to God alone we render worship, but in other things we gladly serve you, acknowledging you as kings and rulers of men."[13]

Whether he realized it or not, with these words Justin injected a deadly dualism into Christianity that continues to plague the church to this day. In effect, he demoted God to overseer of spiritual matters, and crowned Caesar lord over all else. Now the church had two masters, and a Christian's loyalty was torn between them both.[14]

Over time this seemingly innocent dualism grew until, as Christian ethicists Glen Stassen and David Gushee write, "whole swaths of life [were] moved out from under God's authority and placed under the authorities of this world."[15] Pastors and priests grew content focusing solely on getting people into heaven, while the Caesars of this world became increasingly bold in telling Christians what they must do here on earth.

Centuries after Justin Martyr, the Protestant reformer Martin Luther further developed this dualistic reading of Jesus' tax answer into what became known as the doctrine of two kingdoms. To Luther's credit, the doctrine may have been a valid attempt to stop secular rulers from meddling in church life and the papacy from claiming territorial power. Yet even if his intentions were good, the effect of his doctrine was not. Others before Luther had differentiated between the heavenly kingdom and the earthly kingdom, but he took it one step further by claiming that God willed for each kingdom to be governed by a different set of morals. Thus, in their private lives Christians were to obey the ethical teachings of Jesus. But in their public role as citizens of an earthly nation, Christians were to support their political leaders, who governed by way of the sword.

Ultimately, Jesus' tax answer came to mean that Christians have a religious obligation to serve their country. And the most esteemed form of service to one's country became serving in the military. But do you see how far we've strayed from what Jesus' original listeners understood him to be saying? Instead of everything belonging to God, now, as Stassen and Gushee lament, everything but worship belongs to Caesar![16]

Lesson 1: Christlike peacemakers recognize no human law as valid if it conflicts with God's nonviolent love.
Roughly twenty-five years after Jesus gave his famous tax answer, the apostle Paul weighed in on a similar tax debate. And in his reply, Paul stressed that there is one thing we never owe the Caesars of this world.

In Romans 13, having just instructed his readers to "not *repay* anyone evil for evil" (Romans 12:17, emphasis added), Paul turns to the question of paying taxes. It was a timely topic, for in AD 58, a wave of protests broke out in Rome after Emperor Nero revised the tax system. Apparently, the Christians living in the region were tempted to join the uprising.

Paul begins by telling his readers to *submit* to the governing authorities (Romans 13:1). Contrary to how it's often treated, the verb Paul chose to use does not mean to obey. Submission implies accepting the consequences whether one obeys or respectfully disobeys. A classic example of submissive disobedience can be seen in the early Christian martyrs who refused to confess Caesar as lord yet prayed for Caesar's welfare as he fed them to wild beasts.

After advising submission, Paul then addresses the specific issue of paying taxes. His answer employs much of the same language that Jesus used in his answer to the Herodians and Pharisees: "Give to everyone what you owe them: If you owe taxes, pay taxes; if revenue, then revenue" (Romans 13:7).

But then Paul moves beyond the specific issue of taxes and, in effect, draws a line in the sand that he states we must never cross, even if our political leaders demand it. "Owe no one anything," he writes, "except to love one another" (v. 8 NKJV). And just in case love is too ambiguous a concept, he promptly adds, "Love does no harm to a neighbor" (v. 10).

According to Paul, when the Caesars of this world order us to do something that would harm others, we must not obey. As Christians, we owe no one anything but love, the kind of love that never harms another. Of course, we must not confine such love to just our fellow citizens. True love knows no boundaries. It is to be extended to all people, regardless of nationality, race, gender, sexual orientation, or religious affiliation. Thus, whenever a country adopts a policy that benefits some (usually its own citizens or a segment thereof) yet harms others (typically minorities, immigrants, or foreign adversaries), Christian peacemakers must respectfully not comply. In short, no human law is valid if it conflicts with God's all-inclusive, nonviolent love.

SEVEN WOES

Woe to you, teachers of the law and Pharisees, you hypocrites! You shut the door of the kingdom of heaven in people's faces. You yourselves do not enter, nor will you let those enter who are trying to.

Woe to you, teachers of the law and Pharisees, you hypocrites! You travel over land and sea to win a single convert, and when you have succeeded, you make them twice as much a child of hell as you are.

Woe to you, blind guides! You say, "If anyone swears by the temple, it means nothing; but anyone who swears by the gold of the temple is bound by that oath." You blind fools! Which is greater: the gold, or the temple that makes the gold sacred? You also say, "If anyone swears by the altar, it means nothing; but anyone who swears by the gift on the altar is bound by that oath." You blind men! Which is greater: the gift, or the altar that makes the gift sacred? Therefore, anyone who swears by the altar swears by it and by everything on it. And anyone who swears by the temple swears by it and by the one who dwells in it. And anyone who swears by heaven swears by God's throne and by the one who sits on it.

Woe to you, teachers of the law and Pharisees, you hypocrites! You give a tenth of your spices—mint, dill and cumin. But you have neglected the more important matters of the law—justice, mercy and faithfulness. You should have practiced the latter, without neglecting the former. You blind guides! You strain out a gnat but swallow a camel.

Woe to you, teachers of the law and Pharisees, you hypocrites! You clean the outside of the cup and dish, but inside they are full of greed and self-indulgence. Blind Pharisee! First clean the inside of the cup and dish, and then the outside also will be clean.

Woe to you, teachers of the law and Pharisees, you hypocrites! You are like whitewashed tombs, which look beautiful on the outside but on the inside are full of the bones of the dead and everything unclean. In the same way, on the outside you appear to people as righteous but on the inside you are full of hypocrisy and wickedness.

Woe to you, teachers of the law and Pharisees, you hypocrites! You build tombs for the prophets and decorate the graves of the righteous. And you say, "If we had lived in the days of our ancestors, we would not have taken part with them in shedding the blood of the prophets." So you testify against yourselves that you are the descendants of those who murdered the prophets. Go ahead, then, and complete what your ancestors started!

—Matthew 23:13–32

Back when my daughter was learning to walk, she would often stumble and fall. But instead of crying out in pain or asking for someone to comfort her, she'd inevitably erupt in rage, stretch out her arm, and point accusatorily at someone. Whomever she chose to blame usually froze in horror while those spared her wrath struggled to hide their laughter. Only after all her fury had been unleashed would she lower her arm and cease to point.

James Tissot's painting *Woe unto You, Scribes and Pharisees* depicts a similar scene. In it, Jesus is standing authoritatively in the temple, looking down upon the seated scribes and Pharisees. His arm is outstretched as he points an accusatory finger at them. Some of the religious leaders hang their heads in shame while others appear combative. In the background stands a crowd of onlookers, watching with delight as this public shaming unfolds.

Unlike Jesus' tax answer, which contained veiled allusions and cloaked meaning, the Seven Woes are strikingly forthright and unmistakably clear. You don't need a Bible degree to understand what Jesus is saying. With laser precision, he identifies specific ways in which the religious leaders are behaving hypocritically. They hinder local commoners from entering God's kingdom (Matthew 23:13), yet travel great distances to convert prominent individuals (v. 15). They value the temple's gold more than the temple, and the altar's gift more than the altar (vv. 16–22). They obsess over religious minutiae like tithing garden herbs, yet neglect the weightier matters of justice, mercy, and faithfulness (v. 23). They strive to appear righteous on the outside despite having hearts full of wickedness (vv. 25–28). And worst of all, they claim they would not have killed the prophets of old, even as they plot to kill the greatest Prophet of all (vv. 29–31).

Yes, the *content* of Jesus' critique is readily apparent. It is easy to understand. And as such, we don't need to spend more time discussing it. What's less clear, however, is the *intention* behind Jesus' remarks. In other words, what was he trying to accomplish? Are these woes—as Tissot's painting suggests—a scathing critique intent on demonizing a group of religious leaders? Or are they a list of sorrowful warnings aimed at correcting the damaging effects of an immoral leadership?

Many assume the former option. Anti-Semites, for example, have often leveled these charges against all Jews, despite the fact that Jesus was Jewish and limited his critique to a specific group of fellow Jews. Similarly, religious bullies have frequently claimed these warnings give them permission to persecute those they disagree with, even though, as Stanley Hauerwas notes, Jesus spoke his critique from a position of powerlessness to those who had the power to kill him—and did![17]

Yet what if Jesus spoke these woes over the religious leaders not as a judge delivering a guilty verdict but as a parent pleading with his children to turn from their destructive ways?

To put it differently, what if the *intention* behind the Seven Woes is that of restoration, not punishment? At least two factors suggest this is the case:

Ouai

First, it's telling that Jesus began each admonition with the Greek word *ouai*, which we rightly translate as "woe." *Ouai* means to warn sorrowfully. And though violent interpretations of the Seven Woes tend to ignore the latter half of this definition, both halves are central to the word's meaning.

As numerous Greek dictionaries note, *ouai* is an exclamation of grief.[18] The word signifies sadness, not rage. Sorrow, not anger. The emotional heartache associated with *ouai* is clearly seen in verses like Revelation 18:19, which reads, "They will throw dust on their heads, and with weeping and mourning cry out: 'Woe! Woe to you, great city.'"

And when it comes to the word's function as a warning, biblical scholar Alexander Souter adds an important clarification in his lexicon on the Greek New Testament. The word, he writes, "expresses rather a statement than a wish or imprecation."[19] That is to say, Jesus wasn't willing their destruction. Nor was he reveling in an opportunity to curse them. Rather, Jesus was warning the scribes and Pharisees of the state they were in.

Bookends

This understanding of the intention behind Jesus' critique gains further support when we notice the second factor; namely, how the Seven Woes function within the gospel of Matthew as a whole. According to Matthew, Jesus' ministry of public teaching begins with the Beatitudes (5:3–12) and ends with the Seven Woes (23:13–32). Where the Beatitudes start his much loved Sermon on the Mount, the Seven Woes conclude his much avoided Sermon on the Temple Mount. After speaking these woes, Jesus will exit the temple for the last time, never to return again.

At first glance, the Beatitudes and Seven Woes appear to be unrelated. After all, the first list describes the character traits of true disciples, while the latter list critiques a group of immoral religious leaders. Yet a closer look reveals that these two lists actually function as matching bookends to Jesus' ministry of public teaching. The lists seem dissimilar, but only because, like all paired bookends, they face in opposite directions. What the one list condemns is simply the reverse of what the other commends.

The first beatitude declares that the kingdom of God belongs to the poor in spirit, while the first woe accuses the scribes and Pharisees of denying the poor entry into God's kingdom. The Beatitudes teach that the pure in heart will see God, while the Woes assert that hypocrisy has blinded the religious leaders. The Beatitudes call peacemakers children of God, while the Woes admonish the scribes and Pharisees for producing converts that act like children of hell. And finally, the Beatitudes end by blessing those who are persecuted because of righteousness, while the Woes conclude by warning the religious leaders that they are about to persecute the righteous One.

So how does this observation—that the Seven Woes are but the negative image of the Beatitudes—help us identify the *intention* behind Jesus' critique of the scribes and Pharisees? I'd like to submit for your consideration that the two lists are related because they have the same end goal in mind. Both, despite having very different tones, sought to move people in the same direction. And both were spoken in love. To understand how this can be the case, let me offer the following analogy:

Sailing

In the first seminary class I ever took, my professor Gary Deddo likened our experience of God's love to sailing.[20] When you sail in the same direction as the wind, he explained, the whole experience is quite peaceful. Since you're moving with the wind, you feel no breeze. Your boat glides smoothly across the water as it travels in perfect sync with the windswept waves. The sun warms your back, and all is quiet.

If, however, you decide to turn around and head back the other direction, your whole experience suddenly changes. Now the wind roars as you fight against it. Your sail flaps in violent protest. Wave after wave beats against your boat, drenching you to the bone. Cold and wet, you'd swear Mother Nature had just unleashed all her fury on you.

Yet despite how it feels, the weather has not changed in the slightest. The intensity and direction of the wind remain the same. The sun still warms the earth. And the waves continue to be swept along just as they had before. Only one thing has actually changed. And that thing is you. Instead of allowing the wind to lead you where it wills, you've chosen to resist it.

In the Seven Woes, we discover that divine love is like the wind. It's always blowing, always moving, always directing us toward God and a better way of living. Of course, you can turn from God and resist God's love. And when you do, it may feel as if all God's fury has just been unleashed on you. But the truth is, God's love for you has not changed in the slightest. It's still blowing in the same direction. It's still willing your good. The only thing that has actually changed is you. And though God's love now pushes *against* you, it does so because God is ultimately *for* you.

If you think God's love is always nice and kind, that it speaks only encouraging words and never rocks the boat, then you need to read fewer Hallmark greeting cards and more of the Bible. The Scriptures teach us that "the LORD disciplines those he loves" (Proverbs 3:12) and that God "disciplines us for our good" (Hebrews 12:10). That's because when God speaks such judgments over us, God's intention is not to punish us. Rather, it's to bring about our restoration. It's to gather us back to himself.

In fact, Jesus said as much immediately after speaking the Seven Woes. Instead of describing himself as an executioner who had come to bring the sword of justice down on the guilty, Jesus stated that he spoke these warnings because he was like—of all things!—a hen. Like a mother hen trying to gather her wayward chicks under her wing, Jesus was trying to gather a group of wayward leaders back to God (Matthew 23:37).

Lesson 2: Christlike peacemakers speak truth to power and listen with humility when such truth is spoken to them.

When Jesus stood in the temple on Holy Tuesday and warned the scribes and Pharisees of their hypocrisy, he modeled the importance of speaking truth to power. The religious leaders' actions were frustrating God's good intentions for themselves and others. For peace to be restored, their destructive behavior needed to be addressed. In fact, arguably the most unloving thing Jesus could have done in that situation would have been to remain silent. As peacemakers, we must also be willing to speak truth to those in power when their conduct is harming others and destroying shalom.

Admittedly, this peacemaking lesson can be abused, and often is. It's tempting to focus on the splinters in other people's eyes and ignore the plank in our own eye. Yet calling out other people's hypocrisy is not what this peacemaking lesson is about. Many claim to be speaking truth to power, when in reality, they're simply using their authority to bash others. "Christians betray Jesus," Stanley Hauerwas writes, "when they make judgments—like those that Jesus makes against the scribes and Pharisees—from positions of power that transform those judgments into violent and murderous actions rather than attempts to call ourselves and our brothers and sisters to a better life."[21]

Our goal in speaking truth to power should be to encourage the powerful to repent and become agents of healing in our broken world. Those who are in positions of power need to know that if they repent, they will be welcomed in with open arms and forgiven. Indeed, this seems to be what happened after Jesus warned the scribes and Pharisees of their destructive behavior. For, based on their future actions, it appears that at least two of the religious leaders—Nicodemus and Joseph of Arimathea—did repent (see Mark 15:43; John 19:39).

Of course, the reverse of this peacemaking lesson is also true. Those of us in positions of power need to be open to having such truth spoken to us. I, for example, am a white, educated male living in one of the wealthiest and most powerful nations on earth. Regardless of whether I admit it, I am in a position of power. And chances are, if you're reading this book, then you are too. You speak English. You're educated. And you have money and time to spare on books.

To those of us with power, the Seven Woes issue a warning: Don't be so quick to dismiss the powerless when they call out our hypocritical behavior. They don't need to address us with respect. Nor do they need to soften their critique. Jesus did neither when he spoke seven woes over the scribes and Pharisees. Rather, we need to be humble enough to listen to the powerless, consider their warnings, and repent when we've erred.

LITTLE APOCALYPSE

Jesus said to them: "Watch out that no one deceives you. Many will come in my name, claiming, 'I am he,' and will deceive many. When you hear of wars and rumors of wars, do not be alarmed. Such things must happen, but the end is still to come. Nation will rise against nation, and kingdom against kingdom. There will be earthquakes in various places, and famines. These are the beginning of birth pains.

"You must be on your guard. You will be handed over to the local councils and flogged in the synagogues. On account of me you will stand before governors and kings as witnesses to them. And the gospel must first be preached to all nations. Whenever you are arrested and brought to trial, do not worry beforehand about what to say. Just say whatever is given you at the time, for it is not you speaking, but the Holy Spirit.

"Brother will betray brother to death, and a father his child. Children will rebel against their parents and have them put to death. Everyone will hate you because of me, but the one who stands firm to the end will be saved.

"When you see 'the abomination that causes desolation' standing where it does not belong—let the reader understand—then let those who are in Judea flee to the mountains. Let no one on the housetop go down or enter the house to take anything out. Let no one in the field go back to get their cloak. How dreadful it will be in those days for pregnant women and nursing mothers! Pray that this will not take place in winter, because those will be days of distress unequaled from the beginning, when God created the world, until now—and never to be equaled again.

"If the Lord had not cut short those days, no one would survive. But for the sake of the elect, whom he has chosen, he has shortened them. At that time if anyone says to you, 'Look, here is the Messiah!' or, 'Look, there he is!' do not

believe it. For false messiahs and false prophets will appear
and perform signs and wonders to deceive, if possible, even
the elect. So be on your guard; I have told you everything
ahead of time."

—Mark 13:5–23

Immediately after speaking the Seven Woes over the scribes
and Pharisees, Jesus and his disciples exited the temple and
began making their way back to Bethany for the night. By all
accounts, the day had gone quite well for Jesus. He had aced
the religious leaders' unanswerable questions, evaded their
capture, and solidified his support among the masses. His decision to return to the temple had paid off. What had seemed a
death wish proved a victory.

For Jesus' teammates, the stunning upset was cause for celebration. As they departed the temple, the disciples breathed a
collective sigh of relief and began to enjoy the splendor of their
surroundings. "Look, Teacher," one of them exclaimed. "What
massive stones! What magnificent buildings!" (Mark 13:1).
Indeed, even by today's standards, the temple was a marvel
of engineering. Josephus, a first-century historian, wrote that
the largest stones measured seventy-seven feet long, nine feet
high, and ten feet wide.[22] And though Josephus often inflated
his numbers, Borg and Crossan note that archaeologists have
unearthed stones from the temple of similar size.[23]

Given the size of the temple's stones, first-century observers
must have thought the temple complex would endure forever.
And that makes what Jesus said next almost incomprehensible.
"Do you see all these great buildings?" he declared. "Not one
stone here will be left on another; every one will be thrown
down" (Mark 13:2). Comments like that are guaranteed to
suck the life out of a party. No longer in a festive mood, the

previously chatty disciples walk the rest of the way to the Mount of Olives in silence.

Situated halfway between Jerusalem and Bethany, the Mount of Olives offered the perfect location for Jesus and his disciples to pause and rest. As they sat among the olive groves and looked across the Kidron Valley at the temple, Peter, James, John, and Andrew pressed Jesus for more details about his dire prediction. "When will these things happen?" they asked. "And what will be the sign that they are all about to be fulfilled?" (Mark 13:4). Jesus' lengthy answer, known as the Little Apocalypse, warns the disciples of a tragic future filled with suffering, betrayal, and false messiahs. This much is clear. What's less obvious, however, is the specific event being referred to. Was Jesus describing something that would happen to Jerusalem in the near future or some sort of distant cosmic event?

The rapture

Growing up, I was taught that Jesus' cryptic message in Mark 13 described the great tribulation that awaits non-Christians at the end of time. According to this eschatology (which is technically called premillennial dispensationalism), things on earth will—and must—get worse before Christ returns. Christians, however, will not have to endure these dark days, because before things get really bad, God will remove the elect from the earth by a secret rapture. Then, as Barbara Brown Taylor summarizes this eschatological view, "Israel will be restored as 'God's primary instrument in history,' the wicked will be destroyed in the final battle of Armageddon, and Christ will begin a thousand-year reign on earth."[24]

While millions of Christians today embrace this eschatology, the truth is, up until two hundred years ago, no one ever interpreted Jesus' apocalyptic message in Mark 13 in this way. "Whether they know it or not," Taylor explains, "[those who hold this view] owe most of their eschatology to a renegade Anglican priest from Ireland named John Nelson Darby."[25] In the 1830s, Darby traveled the United States, preaching his newfangled rapture theology, which quickly gained a following. Then, in the early twentieth century, Darby's views were launched into the mainstream with the publication of the *Scofield Reference Bible*, which presented Darby's eschatology as undisputed fact. Since then, popular books and movies have continued to expose future generations to Darby's teaching, from Russell Doughten Jr.'s *A Thief in the Night* in the 1970s to Jerry Jenkins and Tim LaHaye's more recent Left Behind series.

While Darby's eschatology focuses—by its very nature—on the future, its effect in the present has been far from neutral. These days, many of Darby's followers get so caught up speculating about the future that they overlook those who are presently in need. In fact, Cyrus Scofield went so far as to denounce working at all for the reformation of society since things on earth will inevitably get worse.[26] Equally destructive, proponents of Darby's eschatology have sometimes claimed a given war is the final battle that Christians must fight in if they want to help usher in the end of the age. And since the end can't come until after Israel regains the Holy Land, many of Darby's followers have become diehard Zionists who uncritically support the modern state of Israel, regardless of how it treats the millions of Palestinians who call the area home.

The Jewish-Roman war

Yet the disciples did not ask Jesus when the world would end. Rather, they pressed Jesus to say when his prediction of the temple's destruction would take place. Thus, to claim Jesus' answer is about the end times, one must strip his response from the question that prompted it.

Despite the popularity of Darby's eschatology within certain Christian circles, biblical scholars almost universally agree that Jesus' apocalyptic message in Mark 13 foreshadows the Jewish-Roman war that took place from AD 66 to 70, which did in fact result in the temple's destruction. Read within this context, we'll come to see that Jesus was teaching his disciples how to stand firm for peace when the world around them erupts into war.[27]

The revolt began in June of AD 66 when Jewish rebels kicked the Roman procurator out of Jerusalem after he plundered the temple treasury. A few months later, Rome sent General Cestius Gallus to quell the insurrection and reclaim the city. It should have been an easy victory for the empire. However, after regaining part of the holy city, Gallus and his thirty thousand troops were forced to retreat when their attempt to retake the Temple Mount failed. Utterly humiliated, Gallus notified Rome of the defeat, while those in Jerusalem praised God for the victory.

But as those who have knocked down a hornet's nest will tell you, some victories only make things worse. In response to Gallus's stunning defeat, Rome dispatched its greatest general, Vespasian, to crush the uprising. After gathering an army of sixty thousand soldiers, Vespasian marched toward Jerusalem and quickly regained the regions of Galilee and Perea. By the summer of AD 68, he had reached the outer walls of the holy city. Yet just when Jerusalem's fate seemed sealed, the unthinkable happened once again. For reasons initially unknown to those holed up in the city, Vespasian abruptly called off the siege and left the region. For a second time, Jerusalem had been spared from almost certain defeat. Surely God was protecting his chosen people.

Eventually the reason for Vespasian's sudden departure became known. Nero had committed suicide, and upon learning the news, Vespasian had left in hopes of becoming the next emperor. He wasn't the only one with such ambitions, however. Three other men were vying for the job, and thus Rome would spend the next year locked in civil war.

Despite the lull in fighting, everyone in Jerusalem knew that Rome would one day return to finish the job. Maybe they'd be back in a month, or perhaps it would take a year. Nobody knew *when* that fateful day would occur, only that it *would* occur. "'Rumors of war,'" Ched Myers writes, "aptly characterizes and describes the way in which news regarding the seesaw political event of AD 68–70 would have circulated around Palestine. Was the siege coming? Were the Romans withdrawing?"[28]

Calling all Jews to fight

During the respite of AD 69, multiple self-proclaimed messiahs and pseudo-prophets appeared on the scene, and they urged all faithful Jews to come to the defense of Jerusalem. To not fight, they insisted, was to turn one's back on both God and country. According to Josephus, these would-be messiahs strengthened their recruitment efforts by claiming recent natural phenomena proved that the end of the age was near and God's final battle against evil was about to begin.[29] Just as Jesus warned, they pointed to events like the severe famine that hit Palestine in the 50s and the earthquake that destroyed Laodicea in AD 60 as proof that God was about intervene (Mark 13:8).

It was around this time that Mark wrote his gospel, and evidently, given his inclusion of the Little Apocalypse, Mark felt compelled to remind his readers of Jesus' apocalyptic warning. As Myers suggests, some Christians may have been tempted to join the rebellion. After all, he asks, "Who could resist the pull of patriotism?"[30] Its allure, especially during times of war, has been known to tear whole families apart, causing "brother to betray brother" and "a father his child" (Mark 13:12).

To those tempted to fight, Jesus' words issue a timely warning. In his brilliant analysis of the war, Myers lists three ways Jesus used his apocalyptic message to counter "the deceptive recruiting slogans" of the phony war messiahs.[31] First, Jesus dismissed their claim that *famines* and *earthquakes* were signs of the end by calling them simply the "beginning" (Mark 13:8).[32] He then went on to warn that "signs and wonders" are the tools used by false messiahs to deceive the masses (v. 22).[33] And finally, Jesus informed his disciples—who asked for a sign—that the only sign they'd receive of being on the correct path is that they would suffer.[34]

"Nation will rise against nation, and kingdom against kingdom," Jesus said. "But . . . they will seize you and persecute you" (Luke 21:10, 12). Who is the *they* that Jesus referred to in this verse? The answer is clear. *They* are the nations and kingdoms that war against each other. And who is the *you* in this verse? *You*, Jesus said to his disciples, will not be part of *them*. *You* will not be counted among those who fight on behalf of their country, for *you* will not participate in their warring. And because of your refusal to fight, Jesus went on to say, you will be hated by all sides (Mark 13:13). You will be "flogged in the synagogues" by your own people, and "arrested and brought to trial" before Roman "governors and kings" (vv. 9–11).

The abomination that causes desolation

After warning the disciples of the persecution they would one day face, Jesus gave his followers explicit instructions:

> When you see "the abomination that causes desolation" standing where it does not belong—let the reader understand—then let those who are in Judea flee to the mountains. Let no one on the housetop go down or enter the house to take anything out. Let no one in the field go back to get their cloak. How dreadful it will be in those days for pregnant women and nursing mothers! Pray that this will not take place in winter. (Mark 13:14–18)

This coded sign—"the abomination that causes desolation"—comes from the book of Daniel (9:27; 11:31; 12:11), where it originally referred to King Antiochus's desecration of the temple in 167 BC. On that day—as you'll recall from our discussion of the event in Palm Sunday's chapter—Antiochus slaughtered an unclean pig on the altar and proceeded to sprinkle its blood throughout the temple.

On Tuesday of Holy Week, Jesus repurposed Daniel's cryptic expression to warn his disciples of a future in which the temple would once again be defiled with blood. While this coded sign could refer to numerous bloody events from the war, one of the more likely options took place during the Passover festivities of AD 70. As Pope Benedict XVI recounts the event, "John of Gischala, one of the rival leaders of the rebellion, smuggled armed fighters, disguised as pilgrims, into the temple, where they began to massacre the followers of his opponent, "Eleazar" ben Simon, and so once again the sanctuary was defiled with innocent blood."[35]

Within days of this event, Rome returned. Vespasian was now emperor, and in one of his first acts, he sent his son Titus to destroy Jerusalem. The resulting siege lasted several months, during which time the conditions for those trapped inside the city rapidly deteriorated. There was looting, arson, disease, and starvation, as well as mass crucifixions. In the end, Jerusalem fell, and just as Jesus had predicted, the temple was destroyed.

Flee to the mountains

Yet because of Jesus' apocalyptic warning on Holy Tuesday, the Christians living in and around Jerusalem were spared this terrible fate. According to the writings of Eusebius of Caesarea and Epiphanius of Salamis, the early Christians heeded Jesus' advice and fled to the mountains.[36] Before Rome returned and the final siege began, a mass migration of Christian refugees is said to have fled to the city of Pella, in the foothills of Jordan.

Within this context, Jesus' seemingly harsh remarks about not "enter[ing] the house to take anything out" and the dread "pregnant women and nursing mothers" will endure make perfect sense (Mark 13:15–17). As has been the experience of countless wartime refugees, these Christians dared not take time to pack. And as many migrants can attest, traveling long distances by foot proved especially difficult for those who were pregnant or carrying young children.

Lesson 3: Christlike peacemakers break the cycle of violence by routinely engaging in small acts of radical love.

Back when the first "abomination that causes desolation" occurred in the temple, Judas Maccabeus called his countrymen to *fight*. But on Holy Tuesday, Jesus repurposed this well-known apocalyptic euphemism in order to call his followers to *not fight*. Instead of participating in the rebellion, they were to flee. That the early Christians refused to take up arms—especially for such a noble cause as the defense of Jerusalem—strongly attests to their rejection of the Maccabean approach to peacemaking.

Yet the call to *flee* was not the only command Jesus gave his disciples when he warned of the temple's future destruction. In fact, if frequency is any indicator, neither was it the most important command. On three separate occasions in our passage, Jesus instructed his disciples to *be on guard* and *watch out* (Mark 13:5, 9, 23). Though translated two different ways by the NIV, in the Greek, it is the same command each time: *blepete*. Be watchful. Pay attention. Stay alert.

In Matthew's gospel, Jesus concluded his apocalyptic warning with a series of parables that underscore the need to be watchful (24:45–25:30). And then, in his final remarks of the day, Jesus specified "the work necessary to sustain those who watch. It is the work of giving food to the hungry," Stanley Hauerwas writes, "and drink to the thirsty, welcoming the stranger, clothing the naked, caring for the sick, and visiting those in prison (Matthew 25:35–36)."[37] Said another way, Jesus was not merely telling his disciples to care for the vulnerable, though that was certainly part of his message. Rather, when read in context, Jesus was warning his disciples that if they wanted to stay awake and avoid becoming entranced by the drumbeats of war, then they must regularly engage in simple acts that cultivate peace. Only those who routinely sow the seeds of peace—small as they may be—find the strength to stand firm for peace when the world around them erupts into war.

A CHANCE TO REST

Tuesday proved to be a long, exhausting day for Jesus. Thankfully, Wednesday will afford him a chance to rest. Yet that doesn't mean nothing important will take place on Wednesday

of Holy Week. On the contrary, numerous life-changing deci-
sions will be made. And we ourselves will be faced with one
such choice.

5

Wednesday

Two Roads Diverged, and I Took . . .

Now the Passover and the Festival of Unleavened Bread were only two days away, and the chief priests and the teachers of the law were scheming to arrest Jesus secretly and kill him. "But not during the festival," they said, "or the people may riot."

While he was in Bethany, reclining at the table in the home of Simon the Leper, a woman came with an alabaster jar of very expensive perfume, made of pure nard. She broke the jar and poured the perfume on his head.

Some of those present were saying indignantly to one another, "Why this waste of perfume? It could have been sold for more than a year's wages and the money given to the poor." And they rebuked her harshly.

"Leave her alone," said Jesus. "Why are you bothering her? She has done a beautiful thing to me. The poor you will always have with you, and you can help them any time you want. But you will not always have me. She did what she could. She poured perfume on my body beforehand to prepare for my burial. Truly I tell you, wherever the gospel is preached throughout the world, what she has done will also be told, in memory of her."

Then Judas Iscariot, one of the Twelve, went to the chief priests to betray Jesus to them. They were delighted to hear this and promised to give him money. So he watched for an opportunity to hand him over.

—Mark 14:1–11

Wednesday—which marks the midpoint of Holy Week— feels like the eye of a hurricane. Jesus has just weathered three tumultuous days—Sunday's crowds, Monday's cleansing, Tuesday's controversies—and soon he will face the headwinds of betrayal, desertion, and crucifixion. But on this particular day, all is quiet. "Too quiet," as pastor David Matthis observes.[1]

Despite the eerie calm, major developments are taking place behind closed doors. The public events of the past three days now give way to private scenes of backroom deals and tableside scandals.

The Gospels divide the events of Holy Wednesday into three interrelated scenes. In each, we encounter a person or group of people grappling with how to respond, given what they've learned over the past few days about Jesus and his way of making peace. Will they offer Jesus their unwavering support, or will they seek to bring about his demise? The first scene focuses on the Jewish religious leaders; the second, an unnamed woman; while the final scene zeroes in on one of Jesus' own disciples.

Today's lull in activity also affords us as readers a chance to pause, consider the implications of Jesus' recent actions, and choose how we will respond. Do we still want to follow this rabble-rouser for peace, or would we be better off rejecting him? At this point in Holy Week, we reach a fork in the road. Two paths diverge—one moves toward Jesus, the other away from him—and before proceeding into the second half of the week, we each must choose which path to take.

As Christians, we often assume we've chosen the route that leads to Jesus. But on this particular day, the gospel writers warn that we may be mistaken. For you see, Wednesday's three scenes are more than just interesting historical accounts. They primarily serve as cautionary tales. We're meant to look long and hard at each of the characters, noticing how their concepts of peacemaking led them to either embrace or reject Jesus, so that we can ultimately determine which character we're actually most like.

We all prefer to identify with those who acted rightly in the Gospels. But sometimes the characters we most admire are the ones we least resemble. As we proceed, pay attention to this distinction, for today's characters function as signposts on the road. By identifying the character you are most like, you'll also discover which path you are heading down. If that's not the direction you wish to go, there is good news: it's not too late to turn back and choose a different way.

We begin with the religious leaders as they meet privately to discuss an urgent matter.

SCENE 1: THE RELIGIOUS LEADERS

According to the gospel of Matthew, on Wednesday morning, "the chief priests and the elders of the people assembled in the palace of the high priest" (26:3). Mark adds that the teachers of the law were also present at this meeting (14:1). Thus, representatives from each of the three groups making up the Sanhedrin were in attendance.

The Sanhedrin was the ruling council of the Jews, comprising seventy members plus the high priest, who at the time was Joseph Caiaphas. Contrary to what you might expect, Rome actually oversaw the appointment and removal of those on the council. As New Testament scholar Craig Keener points out, by filling the council with the members it desired, Rome was also able to obtain the results it desired.[2] Chief among those results were the collection of taxes and the maintaining of public order.

Throughout the year, the Sanhedrin met monthly to discuss pressing matters. And during major religious festivals, while members were already all together in Jerusalem, they held additional meetings as the need arose. Evidently, on this particular day such a need did arise. Thus, early Wednesday morning, the Sanhedrin gathered behind closed doors, and as Matthew records, "they schemed to arrest Jesus secretly and kill him" (26:4).

This much of the story—that the Sanhedrin plotted Jesus' death—is well known. What gets less attention, however, is the *reason* the Sanhedrin wanted Jesus dead. In other words, what motivated the council to take such a drastic step?

As a kid, I was taught that the Sanhedrin were the villains of Holy Week. They were evil men, pure and simple, and their hearts were corrupted by hate. They were jealous of Jesus' popularity, angered by his having challenged their authority, and infuriated that he would call out their hypocrisy in front of the crowds. Their fragile egos could not handle such criticism, so they vowed to kill Jesus.

While such a depiction of the Sanhedrin may make for good storytelling, it's not the reason the Gospels give for why the council wanted Jesus dead. In fact, the Sanhedrin's stated motive was far less sinister and far more pragmatic in nature.

The gospel of John tells us that at the meeting some of the members remarked, "Here is this man performing many signs. If we let him go on like this, everyone will believe in him, and then the Romans will come and take away both our temple and our nation" (11:47–48).

The Sanhedrin saw Jesus as a threat to regional stability. Their fear was not entirely unwarranted. After all, over the past three days, Jesus had riled up the crowds, disrupted the temple's profit-making schemes, and publicly undermined their leadership. The situation was spiraling out of control. And if something wasn't done to stop Jesus, Rome might intervene. The temple—the very center of Jewish life—could be taken away and their nation destroyed.

The gospel of John states that upon hearing his colleagues' concerns, Caiaphas chimed in. But before I tell you what he said, there's something you need to know about the man: Caiaphas was a brilliant high priest, at least in the eyes of Rome. The leadership structure in place in Judea at that time lasted sixty years (AD 6–66). During that time, Rome often replaced high priests. Eighteen different men were appointed to the role, averaging just over three years in office each before getting sacked by Rome. Caiaphas was the exception. He remained in the role for eighteen years (AD 18–36), far longer than any other first-century high priest. The reason Caiaphas stayed in power for so long is that he, better than any of his predecessors or successors, was able to discern the steps needed to maintain stability in the region and thus keep Rome content.

On Holy Wednesday, we witness Caiaphas's political acumen on full display. His colleagues on the Sanhedrin had just identified the problem: There was a miracle worker amassing quite the following. The more miracles he performed, the more people flocked to him. But as his popularity grew, so too did the odds that Rome would intervene. If that happened, the Jewish people might lose their temple and their nation.

The situation was complex. But like Jeremy, my fifth-grade math rival, Caiaphas had an uncanny ability to take complicated word problems and instantly deduce the solution. Having made a quick, political calculation, Caiaphas took charge of the meeting. "You know nothing at all!" he chided. "You do not realize that it is better for you that one man die for the people than that the whole nation perish" (John 11:49–50). With these words, Caiaphas reduced the complex problem down to a simple equation for which the math was indisputable: *one man < an entire nation.*

Lesson 1: Christlike peacemakers contend for peace with means that are consistent with the end goal of peace.

When we vilify the Sanhedrin and claim they killed Jesus out of spite, we conveniently overlook how we are just like them. Notice that Caiaphas never said killing Jesus was a good thing. He simply concluded it was better than the alternative. If a choice must be made between the destruction of an entire nation and the death of one man, the latter was clearly the lesser of two evils. An unfortunate evil, perhaps, but a necessary one.

Caiaphas justified killing Jesus by claiming that his death would prevent an even worse outcome. His argument was a classic case of using the ends to justify the means. This rationale remains the prevailing ideology in our world today for both making and maintaining peace. If police in Hong Kong, for instance, must beat pro-democracy protestors in order to prevent Beijing from cracking down, then so be it. The ends justify the means. If children must be separated from their parents at the border in order to deter foreigners from flooding into our land, then so be it. The ends justify the means. And if Jesus must be put to death in order to prevent the destruction of an entire nation, then so be it. The ends justify the means.

What would you have done if you were one of the Sanhedrin meeting on that fateful Wednesday? Would you have defended Jesus, or would you have joined your colleagues in calling for his death? I'd like to think I would have spoken out against Caiaphas's scheme, that I would never have advocated for the death of the one I now call my Lord and Savior. But I have no grounds on which to make such a claim, for I've often supported my own country's leaders when they've repeated Caiaphas's logic in order to justify their own violent intentions. As painful as it is to admit, when I stare into the face of the Sanhedrin, I see myself.

Recently, however, it dawned on me that Caiaphas's math is not as indisputable as it first seems. His equation actually contains a fundamental flaw. For inherent to the claim that the ends justify the means is the mistaken belief that we can accurately predict what the end result of our means will be. The truth is, Caiaphas could not foresee the future any better than we can. Actions have unintended consequences. Caiaphas concocted a fictional future in which his nation would be destroyed if Jesus was not put to death. Yet in the end, Caiaphas became the very thing he sought to prevent—a destroyer of life. And if anything, his actions only deepened the public's mistrust of the Jewish religious leaders. A mistrust that culminated years later in the overthrow of the Sanhedrin and the start of the Jewish-Roman war. The very war that—as we learned in the previous chapter—resulted in the temple's destruction.

Unlike Caiaphas, Jesus contended for peace with means that were of the same substance as his end goal. His was not—to quote Archbishop Oscar Romero—a peace of violence and of cemeteries, as if peace can be imposed or extorted. Rather, for Jesus, true peace was always the fruit of justice.[3]

One of the greatest temptations we face in working for peace, pastor Brian Zahnd warns, "is to justify violent means by an imagined good end."[4] Give in to this temptation, and there is no limit to the atrocities you might justify. That's not hyperbole. Caiaphas is a case in point.

If you want to be a practitioner of Jesus' approach to peacemaking, then you must learn to see the means you use as nothing less than the end coming into existence. This should not be a profound idea. After all, if you want to grow an orange tree, you must plant an orange seed. And to grow an apple tree, you plant an apple seed. So why would it be any different with growing peace? If you want to cultivate true, lasting peace, then you must learn to plant the seeds of peace. As Martin Luther King Jr. so eloquently preached, "Peace is not merely a distant goal that we seek, but a means by which we arrive at that goal."[5]

SCENE 2: THE UNNAMED WOMAN

Tuesday ended with Jesus telling his disciples how to keep watch, stay alert, and live peacefully in a world at war. Instead of fighting for God and country, they were to engage in radical yet easy-to-do acts of love. Things like feeding the hungry, clothing the naked, housing the stranger, and visiting the sick.

Today, we find Jesus practicing what he had just preached the night before. In stark contrast to the Sanhedrin, who were plotting pseudo-peace from the halls of power, Jesus spent the day in the humble home of a leper named Simon. Curiously, the Bible does not say whether Jesus healed Simon of his leprosy. While past precedents suggest this was the case, perhaps the gospel writers are mute on this point because they want to focus our attention on an even greater miracle; namely, the miracle of a social outcast being welcomed back into community.

And then she entered

Though much could be said about Jesus and his visit with Simon, this scene is not primarily about either man. Rather, the focus is on an unnamed woman and her scandalous act of devotion.[6] The gospel of Matthew states that while Jesus and his disciples were reclining at Simon's table, a woman slipped into the room and quietly made her way to Jesus (26:6–7). Gripped tightly in her trembling hands was an alabaster flask filled with pure nard.

Both the oil and its container were no ordinary household items. Nard was an expensive perfume made from a root found only in the Himalayan mountains. Sealed in a semitransparent, marble-like flask, the substance was likely a family heirloom meant to be left unused so that it could be sold as a last resort to avoid financial ruin. If that's the case, then, as New Testament scholar Ben Witherington notes, this woman was about to use up all her social security for an act of devotion.[7]

Snapping into action before anyone could stop her, the woman broke open the neck of the flask. The sound of cracking alabaster caught everyone's attention. Conversations ceased. Silence filled the room. And the eyes of at least fourteen men locked on to this unnamed, uninvited woman.

With the top of the flask now broken off, the container could no longer be resealed. But that was of no concern for the woman, for she intended to use all its contents. Not a drop of nard would be spared. Without uttering a word, perhaps because of having been silenced all her life, the woman raised the flask over Jesus' head, turned it upside down, and watched as an amber-colored liquid gurgled from the container. It drenched Jesus' hair, ran down his face, splashed off his nose, and soaked his clothes. Simon and his guests stared in stunned disbelief, only to be awakened from their stupor seconds later when a sweet, woody aroma overwhelmed their senses.

A wasted opportunity

According to Mark, as the last drops of nard dripped from the flask, the first cries of outrage filled the room. "Some of those present," he writes, "[began] saying indignantly to one another, 'Why this waste of perfume? It could have been sold for more than a year's wages and the money given to the poor.' And they rebuked her harshly" (14:4–5).

While Mark states vaguely that the reprimand came from "some" in the room (14:4), Matthew pinpoints the "disciples" as the source of the rebuke (26:8). John's gospel goes one step further, singling out Judas Iscariot as the chief complainer (12:4–6). What's more, this was no mere slap-on-the-wrist reprimand. Mark describes the complainers as *indignant* and states they *harshly rebuked* her (14:4–5). Both verbs in the original Greek carry strong connotations. In fact, the latter word, *embrimaomai*, literally means to snort in anger like a horse.

What caused Judas and the other disciples to become so enraged by this woman's act of devotion? Why did they feel the need to accost her? Their stated reason was that the perfume should have been sold and the proceeds given to the poor (Mark 14:5). This may have been what genuinely angered some of the disciples. After all, just the night before, Jesus had instructed them to care for those in need. Plus, it was customary during Passover for the faithful to give alms to the poor.

The gospel of John, however, reveals that at least one disciple, Judas Iscariot, had ulterior motives in voicing this complaint. In an important parenthetical aside, John informs his readers that "[Judas] did not say this because he cared about the poor but because he was a thief; as keeper of the money bag, he used to help himself to what was put into it" (12:6). With thoughts of betrayal now circulating in his mind, Judas no longer needed to ensure that his pilfering from the group's benevolence fund was discreet and undetectable. He could now pocket more than just a few dollars off the top. So of course Judas became irate. The nard was his ticket out. If it had been donated to the cause instead of wasted on Jesus, the perfume would have given Judas the financial means to make a clean break and start anew.

Jesus defended the woman

In response to the disciples' tirade, Jesus promptly defended the woman:

> "Leave her alone," said Jesus. "Why are you bothering her? She has done a beautiful thing to me. The poor you will always have with you, and you can help them any time you want. But you will not always have me. She did what she could. She poured perfume on my body beforehand to prepare for my burial." (Mark 14:6–8)

Like his rebuke of the disciples when they hindered little children from coming to him, here Jesus ordered the twelve to "leave her alone." Their harsh treatment of the woman would not be tolerated. Nor was their interpretation of her actions correct. Far from the woman's act being a scandalous waste, Jesus described it as a "beautiful thing"— in Greek, literally a "good work." According to David Daube, an expert in biblical law, Jesus likely used the phrase "good work" in a technical sense, as Jewish rabbis had created an official list of good works, which included almsgiving, housing strangers, visiting the sick, and burying the dead.[8] In rabbinic logic, preparing a body for burial took priority over almsgiving, since the latter could be done anytime, while caring for the dead demanded one's attention right away.

But why did Jesus equate the woman's act with burial preparation? And what, if anything, is the significance of having nard poured over one's head? The meaning appears to be twofold. First, in the Old Testament, we only read of fragrant oil being poured over someone's head when the person is being anointed king (e.g., 1 Samuel 16:12–13; 1 Kings 1:39). This suggests that the woman considered Jesus to be the long-awaited messiah, the true king of Israel. Second, flasks of nard were customarily used to prepare bodies for burial. As Keener notes, "Archaeologists have uncovered such long-necked flasks in first-century tombs near Jerusalem, suggesting the frequent once-for-all expenditure of this expensive perfume at the death of loved ones."[9] Taken together, these two insights paint a surprising picture, for it means the woman was anointing Jesus as her king, despite knowing he would soon suffer and die.

Perhaps this is why Jesus said, "Truly I tell you, wherever the gospel is preached throughout the world, what she has done will also be told, in memory of her" (Mark 14:9). The woman poured nard over Jesus' head as a memorial to him, but Jesus turned the occasion into a memorial to her. She is to be remembered, for she was the first to understand and accept what Jesus had been saying all along: His efforts to make peace would result in his death, not the death of his enemies.

Three times leading up to Passover, Jesus had predicted his death, only to be met with disbelief from the disciples

(Matthew 16:21–22; 17:22–23; 20:17–19). So at the start of Holy Wednesday, Jesus hammered the point home once more. "As you know, the Passover is two days away," he said to his disciples, "and the Son of Man will be handed over to be crucified" (26:2). Eleven disciples remained in denial, while one finally believed but would soon abandon ship. Ultimately, this nameless woman was the first to understand what awaited Jesus and still support him on his path. In so doing, Marcus Borg and John Dominic Crossan note, she will forever be remembered as the first Christian and a role model to all who now bear the name.[10]

Lesson 2: Christlike peacemakers contend for peace from the margins of society, and from that vantage point they see the true, destructive nature of violence.

Even in the brief glimpse we've been given into this woman's life, we witness her being marginalized in multiple ways. No one asked for her name. No one offered her a seat at the table. And her hesitancy to speak in the presence of men was matched only by the disciples' lack of hesitancy to speak out against her. Yet from her vantage point, having been pushed to the margins of society, this unnamed woman saw what Jesus' disciples could not. It's no coincidence that the first person to foresee how Jesus would be silenced and rejected by society was a woman who routinely endured the same treatment.

My friend Kristin Jack likes to say, "Where you stand determines what you see." It's his way of explaining the power of perspective. If, for example, I look at a can of soup from above, it appears to be shaped like a circle. But when I view that same can from the side, it now appears to be a rectangle. The vantage point from which we view an object affects how we see it.

Situated in the halls of power, the Sanhedrin thought the path to peace required the use of violence. Given where they stood, I'm not surprised they came to this conclusion. They viewed the world from a position of power, and from that perspective they saw the wielding of power as the only real solution to their problems.

Not so with Jesus. Jesus spent his days standing in solidarity with the marginalized. Befriending those cast aside by society (as he did with Simon the Leper) was not a rare practice for Jesus. It was the norm. And defending those harassed by the powerful (as he did on behalf of the unnamed woman) was not a one-off occurrence for him. It was standard practice.

If we're going to contend for peace as Jesus did, we must gain a new perspective on violence by standing in solidarity with the marginalized. Only then will we see the true, destructive nature of violence. Only then will we recognize its inability to produce real, lasting peace. And only then will we see what the unnamed woman saw so clearly: that taking life is never the answer and that having one's life taken is not the worst thing that can happen to you.

Viewing the world from the margins is especially important for those of us who live in powerful nations with massive militaries. As an American, my own perspective on violence changed dramatically when I saw my country's past involvement in Cambodia through the eyes of a refugee:

In 1970, President Richard Nixon and his national security advisor Henry Kissinger devised a plan to help America gain the upper hand in its war against Vietnam. From where they stood in Washington, D.C., Nixon and Kissinger thought they could end the war and bring peace to the region if they ramped up a bombing campaign, begun five years earlier by Lyndon B. Johnson, against Vietnamese troops hiding out in neighboring neutral Cambodia. From 1965 to 1969, under Johnson's administration, the U.S. military had bombed 83 Cambodian sites. But from 1969 to 1973, under Nixon's leadership, American B-52 warplanes bombed a staggering 113,000 Cambodian sites with—according to the Pentagon's own data—an estimated five hundred thousand tons of explosive. That's a blast force equal to the bombings of Hiroshima and Nagasaki fourteen times over.[11]

Sadly, as today's first lesson warned, America's attempt to achieve peace through violent means did not bring about the desired end. Not only did the bombing campaign kill between 50,000 and 150,000 Cambodian civilians, but it also paved the way for a man named Pol Pot and his tiny band of insurgents (known as the Khmer Rouge) to grow in power.[12] In 1973, as America's bombing campaign in Cambodia was coming to an end, the CIA's director of operations sent an urgent message to Washington: "Khmer insurgents (KI) cadre have begun an intensified proselyting campaign among ethnic Cambodian residents . . . in an effort to recruit young men and women for KI military organizations. They are using damage caused by B-52 strikes as the main theme of their propaganda."[13]

Unfortunately, the warning came too late. In 1965, when the bombings began, the Khmer Rouge numbered fewer than ten thousand. By the time America's bombing campaign ended, Pol Pot's forces had surpassed two hundred thousand. Two years later, on April 17, 1975, the Khmer Rouge stormed the capital city, Phnom Penh, and declared the country was to become a self-sufficient, agrarian society. They reset the calendar to "Year Zero," forced city dwellers to farm the countryside, and systematically slaughtered minority groups and intellectuals. By the time the genocide ended in 1979, an estimated 1.7 million Cambodians were dead—one-fifth of the country's population.

One of the casualties was my friend Nay Greenfield's father. After his death, Khmer insurgents forced Nay's mother and aunt to do backbreaking labor in the rice fields, while Nay and her younger brother (who were both under the age of five) were left unattended to fend for themselves. As malnourishment set in, desperation led Nay's mom and aunt to attempt a daring escape. For weeks, the four of them hiked over mountains and through jungles, hiding during the day and traveling only under the cloak of night. Eventually, they reached a refugee camp in Thailand, where they lived for a season before ultimately being granted asylum in New Zealand. Nay became a citizen of New Zealand and spent the rest of her growing-up years there.

Two decades later, as a young adult, Nay and her husband Craig felt God calling them to leave behind the comforts of New Zealand and move into the slums of Cambodia to stand alongside the marginalized and contend for their flourishing. In January 2000, they quit their jobs, boarded a plane, and moved into a little shack in the heart of Phnom Penh. If you were to visit Cambodia today, you'd still find Nay and Craig serving day in and day out among the poorest of the poor. In fact, they've started a beautiful international movement called Alongsiders that connects local Christians with orphans in their own communities (you can read more about Alongsiders in Craig's book, *Subversive Jesus*).

Recently, Nay and Craig opened a camp for Alongsiders on the coast of Cambodia. They named it Shalom Valley. In the center of the camp grounds is a crater—formed by one of the many bombs my country dropped on the region. When construction of the camp began, Nay and Craig had the option to fill in the crater and level the land. They could have hidden this wound from the past. Instead, they chose to preserve it.

And now, week after week, campers sit around the edge of this bomb crater and learn about the peace teachings of Jesus. From the vantage point of this hollowed and now hallowed ground, campers often remark that it's easy to see why Jesus instructed his followers to reject violence.

SCENE 3: THE BETRAYER

The Gospels tell us that as soon as Jesus finished defending the unnamed woman, Judas left to betray him: "Then Judas Iscariot, one of the Twelve, went to the chief priests to betray Jesus to them. They were delighted to hear this and promised to give him money. So he watched for an opportunity to hand him over" (Mark 14:10–11).

When we last saw the religious leaders at the end of today's first scene, you may recall that they had resolved to kill Jesus, yet were unsure of when or how to do so. They feared a riot would occur if they tried to arrest Jesus while the Passover crowds were present. So they resigned themselves to wait until after the festivities ended. Of course, this plan was far from ideal, for it gave Jesus more time to amass supporters.

Sometimes, however, an opportunity arises that's too good to pass up. Such was the case for the religious leaders when Judas Iscariot walked through their door. His arrival must have seemed like a sure-tell sign that God was on their side. The gospel of Luke tells us that with Judas's help, the religious leaders could now monitor Jesus' movements and thus arrest him "when no crowd was present" (22:6).

Why did Judas betray Jesus?

The Gospels never give a direct answer as to why Judas turned on Jesus. Matthew and Mark are completely silent on the matter. Luke simply states that Satan entered him (22:3). Some scholars latch on to John's earlier comment about Judas being a thief and conclude that he betrayed Jesus out of greed. But this conclusion is a stretch for at least two reasons.

First, the Gospels explicitly state that Judas chose to betray Jesus *before* any offer of money was made (e.g., Mark 14:10). It is true that Judas asked the religious leaders what they would give him in exchange for Jesus. But this does not mean Judas's motive was money. It simply reveals that the ever-greedy Judas, having already resolved to betray Jesus, sought to make a profit in the process.

That leads to the second point. If Judas was motivated by greed, it's hard to fathom why he accepted the religious leaders' opening offer. This was a culture in which haggling was the norm. As the only seller of an item the religious leaders desperately wanted, Judas could have set the price. Instead, he accepted their initial bid, despite the fact that they were lowballing him. According to Matthew 26:15, the religious leaders offered Judas thirty silver coins. The specific type of silver coin is not named, but even if we assume the most valuable option—the Tyrian shekel—the silver in the coins would fetch less than $300 today.[14] The offer was a joke—both monetarily and symbolically. Thirty pieces of silver was the price prescribed in the Torah for a slave who had been gored by an ox (Exodus 21:32). By offering Judas this amount, the religious leaders were saying in effect, "We think Jesus is worth no more than a dead slave. Do you agree?" Without hesitating, Judas replied, "Yes."

The only reason you betray a friend for a few days' pay is because you believe that friend first betrayed you. Over the course of the past few days, Judas had come to realize that Jesus was not the kind of messiah he had signed up to follow. On Palm Sunday, Judas watched in confusion as Jesus wept upon a donkey while the crowds hailed him a liberator. On Monday, Judas stood aghast as Jesus drove some of his fellow countrymen out of the temple instead of the Gentiles. On Tuesday, Judas listened in horror as Jesus ordered his followers to not fight for the temple's survival. And finally, on this day, Judas could hardly believe his ears when, not once but twice, Jesus spoke of his imminent death.

If Jesus wanted to die without ever putting up a fight, Judas had no desire to go down in defeat with him. As New Testament scholar David E. Garland writes, "Judas had been ready to commit his life to holy war. Jesus turned out to be a charlatan, and Judas took revenge on him for causing his disappointment."[15] Judas wanted a messiah who would wage peace for Israel by bringing a hammer down on its enemies—just as his namesake Judas Maccabeus had once done. It was now abundantly clear that Jesus would never be that kind of messiah. Jesus had betrayed Judas's expectations, so now Judas would betray him.

Lesson 3: Christlike peacemakers recognize the role that crushed expectations play in triggering violence.

When expectations are crushed, people often turn angry and violent. Parents see this lived out on a regular basis. When I warn my kids beforehand that bedtime is at nine o'clock, they usually go to bed without complaining. But when my kids forget it's a school night and I suddenly dash their dreams of staying up late, a full-blown tantrum is guaranteed to ensue.

What's true of kids is also true of adults. Dashed expectations bring out the worst in all of us. In fact, numerous studies have identified crushed expectations as a leading cause of why people join terrorist groups. The terrorists who hijacked planes on September 11, for example, were not poor, uneducated

Muslims. They were university graduates who were unable to find employment upon returning home.[16] Likewise, most Palestinian suicide bombers during the intifadas of 1988 and 2000 were unemployed college graduates.[17] This pattern—which also holds true of many terrorist recruits in Latin America and white nationalists in the United States—led Christian ethicist Glen Stassen to conclude, "It is not poverty alone but *deprivation relative to expectations* that is a significant factor in the turn to violence."[18]

As peacemakers, we can better identify and address the root causes of a particular conflict when we keep in mind the role that crushed expectations play in triggering violence. Yet today's final lesson also implores us to look inward and examine the role that crushed expectations play in our own tendencies to turn angry and violent. To put it differently, if crushed expectations could lead one of Jesus' own disciples to turn on him, then they could cause us to do the same.

A FORK IN THE ROAD

As I laid out at the start of this chapter, on Holy Wednesday we reach a fork in the road. Two paths diverge. Judas and the Sanhedrin venture down the path that leads away from Jesus, while the unnamed woman takes the route that moves toward him. The only question that remains is, Which path will you choose?

Like the Sanhedrin, will you support the sacrificing of others in order to maintain a status quo that benefits you? Like Judas, will you toss aside those who fail to meet your expectations? Or like the unnamed woman, will you embrace the One who refused to kill yet was willing to be killed?

The choice is yours.

6

Thursday

A Community Conceived

All who enter the eye of a hurricane soon learn that the stillness does not last. Inevitably, the storm's destructive winds return. On Thursday of Holy Week, after a day of relative calm, powerful forces rip Jesus' community apart. One disciple betrays him. Another denies him. The rest abandon him. Today's major events—the Last Supper, Jesus' arrest, and his initial trial—all take place after the sun has set. It's a fitting symbol, for on this day, as Jon Bloom writes, "darkness . . . descend[s] on Jerusalem."[1]

Given the way that Holy Wednesday ended, we should have known the storm would soon return. All three synoptic gospels conclude their coverage of the day with the same ominous warning: "[Judas] watched for an opportunity to hand Jesus over to them when no crowd was present" (Luke 22:6, cf. Matthew 26:16; Mark 14:11).

The most opportune time for Judas to carry out his plan would arguably take place on Thursday evening. At that time, faithful Jews throughout the region would gather together in private homes to celebrate the Passover meal. According to Old Testament regulations, the meal had to be eaten in Jerusalem (Deuteronomy 16:5–6). And given the celebration's elaborate prescriptions, numerous preparations needed to be made. Thus the streets would be empty, the religious leaders could count on Jesus' being in Jerusalem, and Judas was bound to learn the location of the meal far enough in advance to tip off his accomplices.

But this meal was too important for Jesus to allow such an interruption. There was too much he planned to say and do at the gathering. Which is why, under no circumstances, could Judas and his newfound allies be allowed to end the meal prematurely.

Thus Thursday begins with Jesus setting into motion a plan that prevented Judas from learning where the meal would be eaten. Pulling aside Peter and John, Jesus instructed them: "Go into the city, and a man carrying a jar of water will meet you. Follow him. Say to the owner of the house he enters, 'The Teacher asks: Where is my guest room, where I may eat the Passover with my disciples?' He will show you a large room upstairs, furnished and ready. Make preparations for us there" (Mark 14:13–15).

Like a group of fugitives tapping into their network of supporters to evade capture, Jesus sends his two most trusted disciples on a secret mission. In a culture where women were tasked with collecting water, a man carrying a water jar served as the perfect prearranged signal—noticeable to those looking for it, yet easily overlooked by everyone else.[2] "This runner," as Ched Myers aptly describes the man, "leads the disciples to a safe house" where they can prepare the meal and hide from the authorities.³

That evening, once Jesus and the twelve were all together in the upper room, numerous events took place that have profoundly shaped the church's peacemaking vocation. First, Jesus washed his disciples' feet and stated that his followers must empty themselves of power, stoop down, and serve others in similar ways. Then, Jesus infused the Passover meal with scandalous new meaning. If Jesus had been a violent messiah (as so many wanted him to be), he would have torn the bread, poured the wine, and said, "This is my enemy's body. Break it for me. And this is my enemy's blood. Shed it for me."⁴ Instead, as Catholic activist John Dear writes, "Jesus turns that logic upside down and offers a new covenant of nonviolence, saying: 'This is my body broken for you! This is my blood shed for you!'"⁵ After this, Jesus immediately modeled his commitment to nonviolence by warning of Judas's betrayal, yet allowing Judas to leave unharmed. And finally, the gathering ended with Jesus giving his remaining disciples some parting instructions. It's the start of those remarks that we turn our attention to now:

THE NEW COMMAND

When [Judas] was gone, Jesus said, "Now the Son of Man is glorified and God is glorified in him. If God is glorified in him, God will glorify the Son in himself, and will glorify him at once.

"My children, I will be with you only a little longer. You will look for me, and just as I told the Jews, so I tell you now: Where I am going, you cannot come.

"A new command I give you: Love one another. As I have loved you, so you must love one another. By this everyone will know that you are my disciples, if you love one another."

Simon Peter asked him, "Lord, where are you going?"

Jesus replied, "Where I am going, you cannot follow now, but you will follow later."

Peter asked, "Lord, why can't I follow you now? I will lay down my life for you."

Then Jesus answered, "Will you really lay down your life for me? Very truly I tell you, before the rooster crows, you will disown me three times!"

—John 13:31–38

These eight verses, along with the next four chapters of John, are what scholars refer to as the Farewell Discourse. It's a fitting title, for in this section, Jesus informs his disciples of his imminent departure. Like a parent about to embark on a trip, Jesus gathers his disciples around him, tells them he's going away, then summarizes how he expects them to behave while he's gone. "Love one another," he instructs them. "As I have loved you, so you must love one another" (John 13:34). This new command, as Jesus calls it, is what he wants his disciples to focus on when he's gone.

In the heat of the moment, however, the disciples actually ignore Jesus' new command. They instead latch on to the startling news that Jesus is leaving them. Immediately after Jesus gives his new command, Peter interrupts, "Lord, where are you going?" (John 13:36). In the next chapter, three other disciples take turns interrupting Jesus as they, too, struggle to process the news that Jesus is going away. In total, throughout the Farewell Discourse, the disciples interrupt Jesus four times, and four times Jesus redirects their attention back to this new command (John 14:15, 21; 15:10–12, 17).

Eventually, after much time had passed, at least two of the disciples came to realize just how important this command is. How do I know this? For starters, John repeats this command like a broken record in his epistles. In just one chapter of 1 John alone, he refers to it six times. "Let us love one another," John writes, "for love comes from God" (4:7). Soon after, "Dear friends, since God so loved us, we also ought to love one another" (v. 11). A few verses later, "And he has given us this command: Anyone who loves God must also love their brother and sister" (v. 21). And on and on he goes.

Likewise, in his first epistle, Peter repeatedly draws his readers' attention back to this command. "Love the family of believers," he writes (2:17). "Have sincere love for each other," he counsels (1:22a). "Love one another deeply," he pleads (1:22b). And in an attempt to stress that this command tops everything else he has written, Peter concludes, "Above all, love each other deeply" (4:8).

When Jesus first gave this command, the disciples ignored it. But in time, they realized it was of the utmost importance. They're not alone. Out of all the significant events that took place on Thursday of Holy Week, churches across a wide range of traditions have chosen to name the day after this command. Catholics and Anglicans, along with many Protestants and Western Orthodox churches, all refer to this day as Maundy Thursday. The term *maundy* comes from the Latin word *mandatum*. It is a reference to Jesus' new mandate, or as we tend to call it today, his new command.

What makes this command new?
Like the vast energy released by a nuclear reaction, something powerful happens when Christians carry out this command. In fact, contained in this command is a lesson so valuable

that if applied, the effectiveness of your peacemaking efforts will increase exponentially. To discover what that lesson is, we need to answer a simple question: Why did Jesus call this command *new*?

At first glance, there doesn't appear to be anything new about it. After all, love is not a novel concept. This was not the first time Jesus called his followers to love others. He previously said things like "Love your neighbor as yourself" and "Love your enemies" (Matthew 22:39; 5:44). So what makes this command altogether original? The answer is twofold.

The new standard

First, this command is new because, with these words, Jesus has declared himself to be the new standard of love. No longer are we simply to love others as we love ourselves—which is good news, since we often don't love ourselves very well. Instead, for the first time ever, Jesus commands us to love in the same way he has loved us. Our love is to look like his love.

Let's not forget the kind of love we are talking about here. Notice that Jesus does not say, "Love as I have *taught* you to love." This is not a case of the classic bad parenting line "Do as I say, not as I do." On the contrary, Jesus commands us to love each other just as he has actually loved us.

That Jesus makes himself the new standard of love becomes all the more astounding when we consider the timing of this command. Jesus' hands are still wet from washing the disciples' feet when he issues this mandate. His hands are still dripping with the kind of love that sets aside power in order to humbly serve both friend and foe alike. In fact, Judas has just left the upper room when Jesus issues this command. The sound of him descending the stairs could still be heard as Jesus spoke these words. Jesus then uses his very next breath to declare that Peter will soon disown him. And finally, hours from now, Jesus' hands will once again be dripping with love, though this time the drops will be composed of blood, not water. His hands will be outstretched and pierced on a cross, and there, the full extent of his love will be evident for all to see.

In other words, Jesus declares himself to be the new standard of love precisely when his love is being most sorely tried. Perhaps that is why Jesus prefaces the giving of this command with all that confusing talk about glorification. "Now," right now, he says, "the Son of Man is glorified and God is glorified in him" (John 13:31). The synoptic gospels refer to the events of Thursday and Friday as Jesus' *humiliation*.[6] John, on the other hand, sees this moment for what it truly is: Jesus' *glorification*. For in this, his darkest hour, the love of Jesus shines brightest. And it is precisely in this moment that Jesus calls us to love each other just as he has loved us.

The new community

There is a second answer to the question, "What makes this command new?" Though not as obvious as the first, this second answer is just as important. In fact, if Jesus had not added this second element to his command, Christianity as you and I have come to know it would look very different. To grasp the second way in which this command is new, we need to notice the command's communal nature and inward focus. Let me explain:

For starters, it's crucial for us to know that this command is addressed to a group of people, not an individual. In giving this mandate, Jesus did not say, "A new command I give to each of you as individuals." Instead, Jesus used the plural form of the Greek word for "you" throughout this command. To use southern vernacular, Jesus said, "A new command I give to y'all. Y'all must love each other just as I have loved y'all."

It's also imperative that we notice the internal focus of this command. Jesus did not say, "Y'all must love *others*." Rather, he said, "Y'all must love *each other*." Now, you may think I'm being nitpicky. But, in order to see the second way in which this command is new, and in order to unleash the full power of this command, we must take into account both its communal nature and its internal focus.

If Jesus had said, "Each of you must personally love others," it would look like diagram 1. You, as an individual, are the dot located in the center of the diagram. The arrows represent the love emanating from you, and the ring of hollow dots around the outside are the "others" you are loving. Elsewhere in the Gospels, Jesus does in fact call us to love in this way. In the twenty-second chapter of Matthew, for example, Jesus taught, "Love your neighbor as yourself" (v. 39). This diagram is a visual representation of what that command looks like. You, at the center, are extending love to the neighbors around you. Of course, there's a risk associated with loving in this way. You may have noticed that this diagram resembles a star. And the problem with stars is that they inevitably burn out. If you are

Diagram 1.

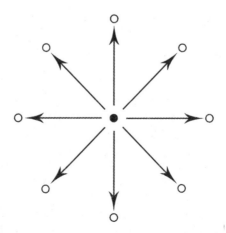

always *giving* love and never *receiving* love, you are a prime candidate for burnout.

That first diagram, however, is not a visual representation of the new love command that Jesus gave on Maundy Thursday. Rather, when Jesus said, "Y'all must love each other just as I have loved y'all," he described a way of loving that looks like diagram 2. For simplicity's sake, I've illustrated what it looks like when four people are committed to loving each other as Christ has loved them. As with the first diagram, the dots represent people and the arrows signify the love being extended to others. But unlike in diagram *1*, here the love flows both ways. Each person is both *giving* love and *receiving* love.

Diagram 2.

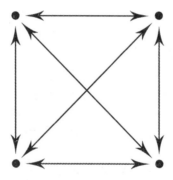

Now that we've connected the dots—pun intended—we can finally name the second way in which this command is new. With this command, for the first time ever, Jesus called his followers to commit themselves to each other. This mandate tasked the disciples with the mission of forming communities that replicate his love. Said another way, when Jesus gave this command, something miraculous happened: the church was conceived. Born weeks later on the day of Pentecost, but conceived on this day.

Imagine what might have happened if Jesus had never given his disciples this new command. On their final post-resurrection day together, after Jesus commissioned his disciples to "go and make disciples of all nations" and then ascended into heaven, the disciples would have stared up at the clouds for a while and then looked around at each other. Given what we know of Peter, I suspect he would have spoken up first. And I imagine him saying something like, "Gentlemen, we've just been given a mission—to reach the nations for Christ. We can cover more ground and get the job done faster if we split up and each head a different direction. Thomas, you take India. I call dibs on Rome. The rest of you fan out. Good luck and Godspeed."

Thankfully, that's not what happened. Instead, in direct obedience to this new love command, the disciples started to form communities whose members strived to love each other just as Jesus had loved them. The first such community began in Jerusalem on the day of Pentecost. According to Acts 2, this community met together daily to pray, share meals, learn from the apostles, and financially support one another. As they focused *internally* on caring for each other, something powerful happened *externally*: outsiders noticed. And soon, new members were being added daily. Of course, this is precisely the effect Jesus said his new command would produce. "As I have loved you, so you must love one another," he instructed, before adding: "By this *everyone* will know that you are my disciples" (John 13:34–35, emphasis added).

Lesson 1: Christlike peacemakers form communities of love that welcome others in so that they can experience Christ's love.

When I lived in the Downtown Eastside, I worked hard to extend the love of Christ to my neighbors. Most days, I walked the streets for a few hours, prayerfully striking up conversations with those camped on the sidewalks. Twice a week, I served breakfast at a local soup kitchen and afterward offered a listening ear to anyone who wanted to talk. I helped convert abandoned lots into community gardens. I regularly attended events at the local community center. And I was always looking for an excuse to treat my neighbors (and myself) to a delicious cup of coffee at one of the many locally owned cafés. Yet if I'm honest with you, I must confess that despite all my personal efforts to minister to my neighbors, I saw very little fruit.

But here's the catch: I didn't move to the Downtown Eastside on my own. My wife and I were part of a missional community of Christians who collectively worked together for the flourishing of those around us. In a neighborhood where loneliness was endemic, hospitality became our community's primary form of ministry. That is to say, we welcomed into our home those who were not normally the recipients of welcome. And once inside, we treated them like family.

We cooked together, ate together, and cleaned the dishes together. We laughed together, cried together, and celebrated even the smallest of milestones together. Many evenings, we'd break out the guitar and sing an eclectic mix of classic rock and classic hymns. Sometimes our neighbors gifted us things. Other times they stole our things. They inspired us and drained us. Blessed us and cursed at us. And often, while waiting to be admitted into rehab, our friends who were homeless came and lived with us.

As we welcomed our neighbors into community, lives were transformed. Many broke free of their addictions and got off the streets. Those who hadn't spoken to family in years began to heal their severed relationships. Several neighbors committed their lives to Jesus. Some even became cherished members of our community. And one neighbor, who joined our community after finishing rehab, is now serving in his eleventh year as a missionary among the poorest of the poor in Cambodia.

Where my personal efforts to love those around me seemed to produce little impact, many of those same neighbors experienced profound transformation when they were welcomed into a loving community. This begs the question, Why did I see such little fruit when ministering as an individual, yet an abundance of fruit when doing so as part of a loving community? What is so special about community? And how do we explain its potential to vastly increase the effectiveness of our peacemaking efforts?

My friend Dave Andrews, who has spent nearly fifty years forming Christian communities among the marginalized in India and Australia, once explained to me the power of community in this way:[7]

One person can *talk* about the love of Christ, and those within earshot can listen. For many Christians, this aptly describes the full extent of their church experience: they show up for an hour each week, listen to a sermon, and then go their separate ways. The best possible outcome of such a scenario is that those who listened will conclude, "Wow! I have just *heard* amazing things about God's love." This is the scenario depicted in diagram 3.

Diagram 3.

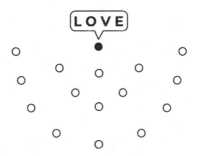

When you have two people committed to loving each other as Christ has loved them, a relationship now exists. Just one. But it's a start. And because of that relationship, these two people can *demonstrate* the love of Christ in the way they care for each other. The best possible outcome of this second scenario is that others will gather around, observe the relationship, and conclude, "No longer have I just *heard* about God's love. Now, I have *seen* it in action." This scenario is illustrated in diagram 4.

Diagram 4.

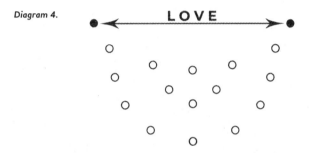

This is a big improvement over the first scenario. Yet something even more profound occurs once you add at least one more person to the mix. Beginning with three people, the number of relationships within the group starts to grow exponentially. With two people, there is one relationship. With three people, there are three relationships. Add a fourth person, and—as diagram 2 in this chapter shows—the number of relationships grows to six.

Here's the point: once you have at least three people who are committed to loving each other as Christ has loved them, a community now exists. And the power of such a community lies in its potential to create a space into which others can be invited so that they might *experience* Christ's love. No longer will they simply *hear* about the love of Christ. Nor will they merely *see* God's love being demonstrated. In community, people can actually *experience* God's transforming love. This is illustrated in diagram 5.

Diagram 5.

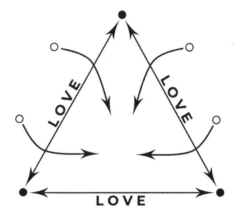

If you want to maximize the effectiveness of your peacemaking efforts, you cannot go it alone. As Catholic theologian Joseph Grassi writes, "Peace is always complete in a community, not within individuals."[8] That's because, on your own, all you can do is *talk* about peace and *demand* justice. But in community, you can actually *embody* peace and *do* justice. Your personal attempts to contend for peace will forever be stunted unless done as part of a community that endeavors to serve in this world as a living expression of that peace. Said another way, Christian peacemakers should strive to form communities that model on a small scale the peace they seek to cultivate on a grand scale. Only then will those who have been marred by violence and injustice be able to *experience* God's transforming love.[9]

THE TWO SWORDS

On December 2, 2015, Syed Rizwan Farook and Tashfeen Malik shot and killed fourteen people in San Bernardino, California, and wounded over twenty others. Two days later, Jerry Falwell Jr.—who at the time was president of the largest Christian university in the United States—stood before his school's student body, gestured to the .25 caliber handgun in his back pocket, and said, "I've always thought if more good people had conceal-carry permits, then we could end those Muslims before they walk in and kill us."[10]

A few days later, in response to mounting backlash, Falwell doubled down on his earlier remarks by appealing to the final command Jesus gave his disciples while in the upper room on Maundy Thursday. Unlike the new love command that we've just discussed, this command was of a very different ethic. Or at least that's what Falwell claimed. "It just boggles the mind," he said, "that anybody would be against what Jesus told his disciples in Luke 22:36. He told them if they had to sell their coat to buy a sword to do it because he knew danger was coming, and he wanted them to defend themselves."[11]

Of all the gospels, only Luke records this shocking conversation between Jesus and his disciples. In a scene sandwiched between the announcement of Peter's upcoming denial and the group's departure to the garden of Gethsemane, Jesus instructs his disciples to acquire swords. Here's Luke's account of that conversation:

> Then Jesus asked them, "When I sent you without purse, bag or sandals, did you lack anything?"
>
> "Nothing," they answered.
>
> He said to them, "But now if you have a purse, take it, and also a bag; and if you don't have a sword, sell your cloak and buy one. It is written: 'And he was numbered

with the transgressors'; and I tell you that this must be fulfilled in me. Yes, what is written about me is reaching its fulfillment."

The disciples said, "See, Lord, here are two swords."

"That's enough!" he replied. (Luke 22:35–38)

As I said in the opening chapter of this book, without Jesus' Palm Sunday lament guiding our interpretation of Holy Week, it's easy to project the week's violence onto God. This passage is a case in point. For centuries, Christian leaders—from Saint Bernard of Clairvaux to Pope Boniface VIII—have echoed Falwell's claim that this text provides a divine endorsement of the right to bear arms. Admittedly, an initial reading of the passage seems to support their interpretation. After all, there's no denying the fact that in this scene, Jesus instructs his disciples to buy swords.

However, when we remember Jesus' declaration from the start of Holy Week that he had come to bring peace, not war, it leads us to question the validity of violent interpretations like this one. For example, if Jesus intended for the swords to be used for self-defense, why did he say two swords were *enough* (Luke 22:38)? Surely two swords shared between twelve men were *not enough* to protect the group from attack. What's more, if the swords were meant to be used for self-defense, why did Jesus rebuke Peter hours later for wielding one of the swords in this way (Matthew 26:52)?

While it's easy to poke holes in someone else's interpretation of Scripture, it's much harder to posit a cogent alternative. If Jesus did not intend for the swords to be used for fighting, we still must explain why he asked his disciples to procure them. In other words, if Jesus truly advocated nonviolence—as I have claimed throughout this book—how do we make sense of this passage?

Some pacifists try to neutralize this scene by claiming that the swords were not actually swords at all. They were cooking knives. The Greek word *machaira*, they point out, denotes a short dagger, not a long-bladed sword. And the presence of two such daggers in the upper room can easily be explained, they say, by the fact that carving knives were needed to serve the cooked paschal lamb.

While this is certainly a clever interpretation, it falls apart when we consider the rest of the story. For as we will soon read, hours later in the garden of Gethsemane, a mob will come to arrest Jesus, and they will be armed with the exact same kind of short-bladed sword (Matthew 26:47). I doubt the mob planned to compete in a barbecue cookoff.

Others who are committed to nonviolence claim that Jesus' final words in this scene should be translated not as "That's enough" but rather as the rebuke "Enough of this!" James Moffatt, a Scottish theologian, was among the earliest to promote this interpretation when his translation of the New Testament was published in 1913. According to this view, Jesus never made the absurd claim that two swords would be enough to defend the group from harm. Rather, when the disciples revealed that they already possessed two swords, Jesus abruptly ended the conversation out of frustration that they had once again misunderstood him. The disciples should have known that his comment about buying swords was sarcasm, or at most, some sort of metaphor.

While this interpretation may be convenient, it too is problematic. For starters, it is quite the linguistic stretch to translate Jesus' final words in this scene (*hikanon estin* in the Greek) as an expression of consternation. Perhaps that is why nineteen hundred years of church history had to pass by before anyone made such a claim. Plus, why would Jesus first remind his disciples of the time he sent them on a mission without *literal* purse, bag, or sandals, only to then speak *metaphorically* or *sarcastically* about buying swords? Only the poorest of communicators would make such a mistake.

What all of these interpretations overlook is the fact that Jesus explicitly states in the passage why he wanted his disciples to acquire swords. Admittedly, the reason is obscured in the NIV since its translators left the Greek conjunction *gar* untranslated. The primary function of *gar*, as New Testament Greek scholar Steven E. Runge explains, is to "introduce the reason or rationale for some preceding action or state."[12] It's typically translated into English as "because" or "for." Thus, if we translate what the NIV left untranslated, the key section reads, "If you don't have a sword, sell your cloak and buy one. For [*gar*] it is written: 'And he was numbered with the transgressors'; and I tell you that this must be fulfilled in me'" (Luke 22:36–37). Why did Jesus want his disciples to buy swords? It was so that Isaiah's messianic prophecy might be fulfilled in him.

What does it mean to be "numbered with the transgressors"? Nowadays, we tend to spiritualize the word *transgressor*. The term has become synonymous in our minds with *sinner*. But the Greek word *anomos*—which is what the NIV translates as "transgressors"—literally refers to a person who operates outside the law. That is to say, Jesus instructed his disciples to buy swords so that he might be counted among the lawless. Because of the swords, Jesus would be labeled an outlaw. Or as the New Living Translation words it: "For the time has come for this prophecy about me to be fulfilled: 'He was counted among the rebels'" (Luke 22:37 NLT). Suddenly, Jesus' claim that two swords were enough makes perfect sense. While two swords were not enough to protect the entire group from attack, they were enough to justify the accusation that Jesus was leading an armed rebellion.

But why would Jesus let others think he was a violent rebel? And why was it so important to Jesus that he fulfill this particular prophecy from Isaiah? The answer to these questions becomes clear only hours later, after one of the swords gets used.

Upon learning that his disciples already possessed two swords, Jesus departed with the eleven from the upper room to make the mile-long trek to the garden of Gethsemane. Once there, Jesus urged his disciples to pray for the strength to resist temptation. But they couldn't even resist the allure of sleep. So Jesus spent the next few hours praying on his own while the disciples slumbered. Then, suddenly, an armed crowd emerged from the darkness:

> While [Jesus] was still speaking a crowd came up, and the man who was called Judas, one of the Twelve, was leading them. He approached Jesus to kiss him, but Jesus asked him, "Judas, are you betraying the Son of Man with a kiss?"
>
> When Jesus' followers saw what was going to happen, they said, "Lord, should we strike with our swords?" And one of them struck the servant of the high priest, cutting off his right ear.
>
> But Jesus answered, "No more of this!" And he touched the man's ear and healed him.
>
> Then Jesus said to the chief priests, the officers of the temple guard, and the elders, who had come for him, "Am I leading a rebellion, that you have come with swords and clubs? Every day I was with you in the temple courts, and you did not lay a hand on me. But this is your hour—when darkness reigns." (Luke 22:47–53)

In this second half of the two-sword saga, we witness the fulfillment of Isaiah's prophecy. Those in the crowd that came to arrest Jesus in the garden clearly misunderstood who he was. They showed up armed with clubs and swords, expecting a fight. They assumed force would be necessary to arrest Jesus because, just as Isaiah prophesied, they wrongly believed he was leading a rebellion.

Upon seeing the armed crowd, the disciples asked, "Lord, should we strike with our swords?" (Luke 22:49). It was a reasonable question, for as John Dear notes, "If ever there was a moment in God's eyes when violence would be justifiable, this is it!"[13] Here was a violent mob threatening an innocent man. And though the disciples hadn't gone looking for a fight, who could blame them for refusing to back down from one? Yes, the right thing to do was obvious. And so, despite asking Jesus for permission to fight, the disciples never actually waited for his answer. One of them (whom the gospel of John identifies as Peter) drew his sword and hacked off the ear of the high priest's servant.

I'm not surprised that of all the people present in the crowd, it was a servant—forced to do his master's dirty work—who bore the brunt of the violence. You don't have to live long among the poor and powerless before you begin to understand why they are disproportionately affected by violence. It's not just that they are more frequently the victims of violence, though that is true. It's also that they are the primary ones conscripted by the powerful to do their fighting. In the United States, for example, I have lived in poor sections of three cities: Philadelphia, Wichita, and Los Angeles. In each, my home was within walking distance of at least one military recruiting office. Most weeks, recruiters could be seen walking the streets trying to enlist my neighbors. When was the last time you saw military recruiters going door-to-door in the suburbs?

As soon as Peter chopped off the servant's ear, and before the violence could escalate any further, Jesus intervened. "No more of this!" he shouted with an air of authority that stopped everyone in their tracks, thus proving that words can be more powerful than swords (Luke 22:51). And then, while all were watching, Jesus repaired the damage caused by Peter's violence. He healed the servant's ear.

According to the gospel of Luke, Jesus then turned to the chief priests, temple guard, and elders (i.e., the leaders of the mob), and he contrasted his public actions in the temple with the fact that they were sneaking around in the dark of night armed with weapons (22:52–53). In other words, as Joseph Grassi summarizes, "They are the violent ones, not he."[14] In Matthew's gospel, Jesus also directly addressed Peter. As soon as Peter chopped off the servant's ear, Jesus turned to his disciple and said, "Put your sword back in its place, for all who draw the sword will die by the sword" (Matthew 26:52).

Lesson 2: Christlike peacemakers exchange their weapons of war for tools that cultivate life and healing.

Herein lies the answer to our earlier questions, Why did Jesus tell his disciples to buy swords? And why did he temporarily allow others to assume he was a rebel? Because it gave Jesus an opportunity to unequivocally, once and for all, denounce the use of violence. As Brian Zahnd explains, "Jesus did not arm his disciples so they could fight; Jesus armed his disciples so that prophecy would be fulfilled and so that he could disarm them!"[15]

Some scholars claim that Jesus rebuked Peter not because it was wrong of Peter to use a weapon in self-defense but because he was thwarting God's plan of redemption.[16] Jesus had to die on a cross, they say, and Peter could not be allowed to interfere. But such an interpretation twists Jesus' logic. As Moyer Hubbard, professor of New Testament language and literature, notes, Jesus' rebuke of Peter "is not a 'the time is not right' kind of prohibition; it is a 'the time is never right' kind of prohibition."[17] After ordering Peter to put his sword away, Jesus declares a new universal law, one that has proven true throughout time and place. "All who draw the sword will die by the sword" (Matthew 26:52b). Said another way, all who rely on violence to advance their agenda in the world will ultimately be destroyed by violence.

The earliest Christians were staunch pacifists, and they often referred to Jesus' rebuke of Peter to explain their refusal to fight. Perhaps nobody articulated the point more memorably than Tertullian, a prolific second- and third-century author from Carthage. "In disarming Peter," he wrote, "Christ disarmed every soldier."[18] Other early Christian writers found it deeply significant that Jesus' condemnation of violence took place in a garden. They saw in this the fulfillment of an ancient prophecy—spoken of by Isaiah, Joel, and Micah—that envisioned a day when people would convert their weapons of war into garden tools (cf. Isaiah 2:4; Joel 3:10; Micah 4:3). Picking up on this imagery, Justin Martyr wrote of the early church, "All of us throughout the whole wide earth have traded in our weapons of war. We have exchanged our swords for plowshares and our spears for farm tools."[19] Whereas weapons are designed to kill and destroy, garden tools are used to cultivate life.

In the garden on Maundy Thursday, Jesus forever forbade his followers from using violence. Immediately after, he healed the servant's ear. Likewise, it is not enough for us to lay down our weapons of war; we must also strive to be God's instruments of peace in this world. Entrusting our lives to the Master

Gardener, we contend each day for the healing and flourishing of our neighbors.

THEN EVERYONE DESERTED HIM

When the mob arrived armed with clubs and swords to arrest Jesus, the disciples stayed by his side. They were ready to kill for Jesus, and perhaps even to die for him. But as soon as the disciples realized that Jesus refused to fight, Mark writes, "Then everyone deserted him and fled" (14:50). As John Dear notes, "This nonviolent Jesus [was] more than they had bargained for."[20] In fact, Mark states that one of them, out of desperation to get away from Jesus and his captors, "fled naked, leaving his garment behind" (14:51–52). Talk about a tragic turn of events. As theologian Edward Sri explains, at the start the disciples left everything to follow Jesus (Mark 10:28). But now, one of them left everything behind in order to stop following Jesus.[21] Perhaps some of us are also looking for the closest exit.

As an icy chill fills the air, the mob arrests Jesus. They will drag him first before Annas (the former high priest) and then deliver him to Caiaphas (the current high priest). There, the Sanhedrin will conduct a sham trial as they seek false evidence to justify having Jesus executed. Those guarding Jesus will mock him and beat him. Others will spit in his face. Most painful of all, Jesus will overhear Peter deny knowing him three times. With that, Thursday night comes to a close, and we are left with the sinking feeling that hate has won.

7

Friday

Who Holds the Hammer?

"God the Father is like a hammer," the camp speaker declared as he held a large mallet up for all the kids to see.

He then reached into his box of props and pulled out a drinking glass. "Each of us," the man continued, "is like this glass full of dirty water. We are all filthy, wretched sinners."

Placing the glass on the table in front of him, the evangelist took a pair of safety glasses out of his pocket and put them on. "Students," he said, "I hope you never forget what I'm about to teach you. Our heavenly Father is holy and just. And because of that, he cannot let our sins go unpunished."

Then, as all the campers watched in horror, the man raised the hammer high above his head and proceeded to bring it crashing down toward the glass. Those sitting in the front row shielded their faces in anticipation of the glass shards that would soon be flying toward them. At the last possible second, however, the camp speaker diverted the path of the hammer, causing it to narrowly miss its target.

"We deserve for God to destroy us," he continued. "But in an act of pure grace, Jesus came to earth in order to save us from his Father's wrath." He then pulled the last prop out of his box—a large metal bucket. Turning it upside down, he placed it over the drinking glass and said, "Like this bucket, Jesus is our protective shield."

Then, in a dramatic conclusion that none would soon forget, the speaker began pounding the bucket with the hammer as he yelled, "So God the Father"—*whack*—"satisfied his just wrath"—*whack*—"by unleashing the punishment we deserve"—*whack*—"upon his Son"—*whack*.

Decades later, my seminary classmates and I sat in stunned disbelief as our theology professor Gary Deddo recounted this episode from his childhood.[1] At the time, he said, the speaker's evangelistic demonstration proved highly effective. I'm not surprised. Whacking a metal bucket with a hammer is guaranteed to bring a dead audience to life. If your goal is to scare the hell out of people (in either sense of the phrase), then this is the demonstration to use. When the speaker finished his message and gave the altar call, Deddo told us that scores of campers flooded to the front to be saved.

But since when is the gospel message "Cling to Jesus so he can save you *from God*"?

THE FIRST TIME A CROWD TRIED TO KILL JESUS

While writing this book, I've often reflected on a piece of sage advice Brian Zahnd once gave. When it comes to the cross, he counseled, "let's readily confess it, but never glibly explain it."[2] As Christians, we should all be quick to confess, as Paul did, that on the cross Jesus won our peace (Colossians 1:20). Yet it's foolhardy to think, as the camp speaker did, that we can easily explain with a few household items *how* the crucifixion of Jesus achieved this feat.

Many of our misconceptions about the cross flow from an inadequate understanding of what Jesus sought to accomplish on earth. It's not that our understanding of Jesus' mission is necessarily incorrect; it's just incomplete. So to safeguard against harmful misinterpretations of the cross, before we consider the events of Good Friday, we're first going to go back to the start of Jesus' public ministry, to the day when he publicly declared what his messianic mission would be all about. In response to his announcement, those listening tried to kill him. The incident is recorded in the second half of Luke 4, though the previous chapters provide much-needed context.

The first three chapters of Luke tell the story of Jesus' birth and growing-up years. Woven into these chapters are four firsthand accounts from four first-century Jews that reveal what they thought the messiah was coming to do. Zechariah envisions the messiah as a national liberator (Luke 1:67–79). John the Baptist anticipates him leveling the playing field (3:3–6). Mary sings of the messiah toppling rulers from their thrones (1:46–55).[3] And Simeon refers to him as the glory of Israel (2:25–32).

After revealing what most first-century Jews expected the messiah to be like, Luke writes that Jesus went out into the desert, where he was tempted by the devil to become the kind of messiah everyone wanted him to be. He refused. Emboldened by the experience and empowered by the Spirit, Jesus then returned to his hometown of Nazareth and entered the synagogue. There, he launched his public ministry with an inaugural address that laid out, in no uncertain terms, what his messianic agenda would be all about. Having been handed the scroll of Isaiah, Jesus stood before his former neighbors and read aloud:

> The Spirit of the Lord is on me,
>   because he has anointed me
>   to proclaim good news to the poor.
> He has sent me to proclaim freedom for the prisoners
>   and recovery of sight for the blind,
>   to set the oppressed free,
>   to proclaim the year of the Lord's favor.
> (Luke 4:18–19)

After reading these words, Jesus took a long, dramatic pause. He rolled up the scroll, handed it back to the attendant, and sat down, all without uttering a word. Luke states that "the eyes of everyone in the synagogue were fastened on him" (4:20). Of course Jesus had everyone's attention. He'd just read one of the most famous messianic texts in all the Hebrew Scriptures.[4] So understandably, when Jesus chose to read this cherished passage, everyone's ears perked up. "Is Jesus saying what I think he's saying?" some likely wondered. And let's not forget that this was Jesus' hometown. Many were probably thinking to themselves, "Oh my goodness! The rumors are true. Mary's son really is the messiah!"

Sure enough, seconds later their wildest dreams come true. Luke writes that Jesus "began to say to them, 'Today this Scripture is fulfilled in your hearing'" (4:21 NKJV). Translation: "I am the long-awaited messiah." At this, the crowd erupted in celebration. They didn't even let Jesus finish his remarks (hence Luke's wording that Jesus had only *begun to speak*). Luke writes that the people, having cut Jesus off mid-message, "all spoke well of him," for they were "amazed at the gracious words that came from his lips" (4:22).

Over the years, I've heard numerous pastors preach on this passage. "If Jesus was anointed to bring good news to the poor, imprisoned, and oppressed," they taught, "then this needs to be our mission as well." I wholeheartedly agree. Yet it's important to note that Jesus' original listeners did not interpret his message in this way. They describe his words as being *gracious*. And the only reason you do that is if you consider yourself to be the recipient of that grace. In other words, when Jesus declared that he had come to help a specific group of marginalized people, his listeners thought to themselves, "That's us! He's talking about us. We're the poor ones who have been oppressed and imprisoned by the Romans."

The last line Jesus read further confirmed their interpretation of his message. "The year of the Lord's favor" is a reference to the year of Jubilee. That's when, according to the Old Testament, land gets restored and the enslaved get set free. No wonder Luke says they all spoke well of Jesus. They thought he was going to retake their land and win their freedom.

This was really good news. Well, it was bad news for the Romans. But that just made it even better news for Jesus' listeners. So far, so good. The people of Nazareth loved Jesus' message. They loved it, that is, until he went on to clarify that his mission was not just for them.

> "Truly I tell you," he continued, "no prophet is accepted in his hometown. I assure you that there were many widows in Israel in Elijah's time, when the sky was shut for three and a half years and there was a severe famine throughout the land. Yet Elijah was not sent to any of them, but to a widow in Zarephath in the region of Sidon. And there were many in Israel with leprosy in the time of Elisha the prophet, yet not one of them was cleansed—only Naaman the Syrian." (Luke 4:24–27)

"You think I've come to benefit only you," Jesus said in essence, "yet my mission extends to even the most marginalized of outsiders, like the foreign widow Elijah helped." If that wasn't infuriating enough, Jesus then went one step further, or as his listeners would conclude, one step too far. For you see, Naaman was not just any foreigner. Naaman was a commander in an enemy nation's army.

In less than a minute, the crowd went from loving Jesus to hating him. Luke writes that as soon as Jesus mentioned Naaman,

> all the people in the synagogue were furious when they heard this. They got up, drove him out of the town, and took him to the brow of the hill on which the town was built, in order to throw him off the cliff. But he walked right through the crowd and went on his way. (4:28–30)

If Jesus *only* came to earth to die for our sins so that we might have life—which is what I was taught in Sunday school—then he didn't need thirty-three years to accomplish this mission. He didn't even need a week. Jesus could have incarnated as an adult and then—as Luke 4 reveals—simply delivered a contentious message, infuriated his listeners, and gotten tossed to his death. Mission accomplished. All in ten minutes or less!

In fact, getting thrown off a cliff would have been a death filled with rich spiritual meaning. Every year on the Day of Atonement—when the people of Israel collectively made amends for their sins—the high priest would take a goat, lay his hand on its head, and confess all the sins of Israel, thus transferring those sins onto the animal. This scapegoat was then led out of the city and left in the barren wilderness to die. Over time, however, a problem emerged. On more than one occasion, the goat—the very embodiment of Israel's sins—ventured back into the city. Adults gasped, children giggled, and priests began to plot how to prevent this from happening again. To remedy the situation, a new tradition emerged. From then on, the goat was taken out of the city and killed by being tossed off a cliff.[5]

So if dying for our sins was Jesus' sole mission, then getting hurled over a cliff would have been an ideal way to die. Jesus would forever be remembered as the perfect, once-and-for-all scapegoat who bore our sins and died in our place. Our hymns would speak of kneeling at the foot of the cliff. We'd have images of dead goats tattooed on our arms. And once a year, our congregations would gather outside to watch our pastors toss stuffed billy goats off the church roof.

Yet according to Luke, when the crowd tried to throw Jesus off a cliff, he passed through the midst of them and went on his way (4:30). Apparently, Jesus was not ready to die at that time. It seems there was more he wanted to accomplish before laying down his life.

The significance should not be lost on us that Jesus had an opportunity to die like a scapegoat on the Day of Atonement, yet he chose instead to lay down his life on Passover. The Day of Atonement is about forgiveness. Passover, on the other hand, is about liberation. On the first Passover, God liberated the people of Israel from Egyptian enslavement. But giving the Israelites their life back was only the beginning of their liberation journey. They spent the next forty years wandering the desert as God worked tirelessly to liberate them from their harmful ways of living and mistaken beliefs about what God is like.

All three elements were also part of Jesus' liberating mission on earth. This is why Jesus referred to himself as "the way and the truth and the life" (John 14:6). Yes, Jesus died for our sins so that we might have *life*. But he also came to show us the *way* to live and the *truth* about God. While the first task could have been accomplished quickly (as Luke 4 indicates), the latter two tasks required Jesus to spend years living among us.

In Jesus, we discover what it looks like to live as a child of God. Jesus is the archetype of humanity, the Human One, the true Adam who perfectly models how to live. When we overlook this core part of Jesus' mission, we risk divorcing the cross from the way of life that led to it. Most books on Holy Week, for example, dedicate a disproportionate number of pages to Good Friday. That's understandable, yet the gospel writers did the opposite. They frontloaded their coverage of Holy Week, dedicating just 6 percent to the crucifixion. Why? Because the cross is more than just something Jesus endured for our sake (as important as that is); it is also the end result of a way of living we are called to imitate.

Jesus also came to earth to set the record straight, once and for all, about what God is like. The Scriptures teach that Jesus is the definitive revelation of God (Hebrews 1:3), the clearest image of what God is like (Colossians 1:15), literally God in the flesh (John 1:14). Thus, if you want to know what God is like, if you want to discover the very heart and character of God, look to Jesus. When we overlook this core part of Jesus' mission, we risk explaining the atoning work of the cross in ways that pit the Father against the Son. This is precisely what the camp speaker did when he claimed that God is like a hammer. Unlike his glib explanation of the crucifixion, the Scriptures teach us that it was because "God so *loved* the world that he gave his one and only Son" (John 3:16, emphasis added), and that on the cross, "God was in Christ reconciling the world to Himself" (2 Corinthians 5:19 NKJV).

So if God is not like a hammer, what is God like? And if God was not the one holding the hammer, who was? Now that we have a better understanding of Jesus' earthly mission, we can safely discuss the events of Good Friday. But before we do, I want to highlight an important peacemaking lesson from Luke 4, for it will also aid our efforts to make sense of Jesus' actions on Good Friday.

Lesson 1: Christlike peacemakers live by a spirit of mercy, never vengeance.

When Jesus stood in his hometown synagogue and read from the scroll of Isaiah, he chose to stop reading at a peculiar place. In our modern English Bibles, Jesus stops midsentence, not even at a comma. In its entirety, the final line from Isaiah 61:2 reads, "To proclaim the year of the LORD's favor and the day of vengeance of our God." Jesus left off the part his listeners would have enjoyed the most. He omitted the reference to divine vengeance against Israel's enemies.

Normally, we shouldn't make too much of an omission. After all, Jesus had to stop reading from the scroll at some point. Yet this is not the only time when Jesus omitted references to divine vengeance when quoting from the Hebrew Scriptures. In Luke 7:22, for instance, he removed all talk of vengeance from three passages in Isaiah (35:4–5; 29:18–20; 61:1–2) and then fused together the remaining content. "This can hardly be unintentional," missiologist David Bosch concludes.[6]

Furthermore, in the second half of his Luke 4 sermon, Jesus revealed that his mission would be the opposite of vengeance. Elijah and Elisha were not exactly famous for extending mercy to others, especially to outsiders. Elijah, as you may recall, once slaughtered 450 prophets of Baal. And Elisha once cursed a group of teens after they mocked his bald head. Thus, it's highly significant that Jesus chose to make normative two rare instances of Elijah and Elisha showing mercy to outsiders.

Jesus avoided all talk of vengeance because he came on a mission of pure mercy. Likewise, he calls his followers to also be a people of mercy. Always mercy. Never vengeance. Before grasping this truth, the disciples often failed to exude mercy. Back when a Samaritan village refused to welcome Jesus, for example, two of the disciples asked, "Lord, do You want us to command fire to come down from heaven to consume them, just as Elijah did?" (Luke 9:54 NKJV). Despite their appeal to Old Testament precedent, Jesus rebuked them, stating, "You do not know what manner of spirit you are of. For the Son of Man did not come to destroy men's lives but to save them" (Luke 9:55–56 NKJV).

Like the two disciples, we often forget what manner of spirit Christ followers are meant to be of. It's so easy for us to slip into the base ethic of this world, to live by a spirit of vengeance in which we impart to others what we believe they deserve. But Jesus calls us to live by a spirit of mercy (Luke 6:36). Getting even should never be our goal. Rather, no matter what others do to us—whether good or bad—when we live by a spirit of mercy, our aim should be to treat others in ways that promote their healing and wholeness.

When it comes to peacemaking, living by a spirit of mercy makes all the difference in the world. For example, when the media bombards us with the message "Undocumented immigrants don't *deserve* our help," Christian peacemakers will be quick to reframe the conversation, asking instead how their churches can extend *mercy* to the strangers in their midst.

And when our nations declare (as they often do), "This war is *justified*," Christian peacemakers will respond, "Even if it is justifiable, no war will ever be *merciful*." That's why Christian peacemakers labor for peace in ways that seek the loving restoration of all people, even enemies.

As we turn now to the events of Good Friday, pay close attention to people's actions, and ask yourself, Are they motivated by a spirit of vengeance or a spirit of mercy?

JESUS STANDS TRIAL BEFORE PONTIUS PILATE

Very early in the morning, the chief priests, with the elders, the teachers of the law and the whole Sanhedrin, made their plans. So they bound Jesus, led him away and handed him over to Pilate.

"Are you the king of the Jews?" asked Pilate.

"You have said so," Jesus replied.

The chief priests accused him of many things. So again Pilate asked him, "Aren't you going to answer? See how many things they are accusing you of."

But Jesus still made no reply, and Pilate was amazed.

Now it was the custom at the festival to release a prisoner whom the people requested. A man called Barabbas was in prison with the insurrectionists who had committed murder in the uprising. The crowd came up and asked Pilate to do for them what he usually did.

"Do you want me to release to you the king of the Jews?" asked Pilate, knowing it was out of self-interest that the chief priests had handed Jesus over to him. But the chief priests stirred up the crowd to have Pilate release Barabbas instead.

"What shall I do, then, with the one you call the king of the Jews?" Pilate asked them.

"Crucify him!" they shouted.

"Why? What crime has he committed?" asked Pilate.

But they shouted all the louder, "Crucify him!"

Wanting to satisfy the crowd, Pilate released Barabbas to them. He had Jesus flogged, and handed him over to be crucified.

—Mark 15:1–15

As you'll recall from the close of the previous chapter, after being arrested in the garden of Gethsemane, Jesus stood trial before Caiaphas and the Sanhedrin. Having manufactured evidence, they charged him with blasphemy, which according to Jewish law deserved the death penalty. If this incident had occurred a few years earlier, they could have executed Jesus on their own. But now, they faced a problem. According to historical records, Rome had recently rescinded the Jewish people's right to execute anyone.[7] In order to have Jesus put to death, the Sanhedrin needed Pilate's approval. Thus, early Friday morning, having beaten and bound Jesus, they dragged him before Pontius Pilate.

Knowing Pilate had no interest in mediating internal Jewish religious disputes, the Jewish council presented charges not of blasphemy but of something much more relevant to Pilate's interests: "We have found this man subverting our nation," they said. "He opposes payment of taxes to Caesar and claims to be Messiah, a king" (Luke 23:2). In short, they accused Jesus of sedition.

In response to the accusation, Pilate turned to Jesus and asked, "Are you the king of the Jews?" (Luke 23:3). We tend to interpret Pilate's question as if he was genuinely interested in learning the answer. But the original Greek suggests the emphasis falls on the word *you*. In other words, Pilate could hardly believe that the pitiful excuse of a man standing before him could ever be guilty of such a charge. "*You* are the king of the Jews?" he asked incredulously. "*You*—who stand before me beaten, bloodied, and rejected by your own people—claim to be their king?"

In reply, Jesus gave a cryptic nonanswer: "You have said so" (Luke 23:3). According to the synoptic gospels, this terse response is the only comment Jesus made while standing accused before Pontius Pilate. In John's gospel, however, Pilate pressed Jesus further. "What is it you have done?" he asked (18:35). To which Jesus replied, "My kingdom is not of this world. If it were, my servants would fight to prevent my arrest by the Jewish leaders" (John 18:36). With these words, Jesus both acknowledged that he was a king and insisted—as he'd done throughout Holy Week—that his kingdom was not advanced through force.

Which messiah will you choose?

What happened next is recorded in all four gospels, which indicates just how important it is to understanding the events of Good Friday. The gospel writers all state that it was Pilate's custom during Passover to let the Jewish people choose one prisoner to release. Though the Gospels paint a largely sympathetic picture of Pilate, other historical writings from the time describe him as "inflexible, merciless and obstinate."[8] His custom of releasing a prisoner during Passover was likely not an act of compassion, but rather a calculated strategy aimed at placating the Jewish people during a week when tensions were high.

The Gospels differ on who initiated the request that a prisoner be released. Mark and Luke state that the crowd asked Pilate to uphold his usual custom (Mark 15:8; Luke 23:18). Matthew and John, on the other hand, have Pilate initiating the offer (Matthew 27:17; John 18:39). Regardless, what all four gospels do agree on is that the choice of whom to release came down to Jesus and a prisoner named Barabbas. This choice represents the fundamental decision all of us must make on Good Friday. But we cannot understand the significance of this choice unless we can first answer two questions: What crime did Barabbas commit? And what is the meaning of his name?

As to the crime: Barabbas was not in jail for a petty misdemeanor. Nor was he serving time because he couldn't pay off a debt. He was not a common thief, a convicted swindler, or some sort of criminal mastermind. Many have claimed that Barabbas was imprisoned for murder. While this is partly true, such a charge overlooks the context in which the murder took place. Mark, Luke, and John all state that Barabbas was an insurrectionist who murdered someone in a past uprising (cf. Mark 15:7; Luke 23:19; John 18:40). In other words, Barabbas was a violent revolutionary—albeit a failed one—but at least he had proven his willingness to fight for Israel's liberation.

The name Barabbas is also significant. It means "son of Abba"—that is to say, son of the Father. What's more, the gospel of Matthew provides us with his full name. "Which one do you want me to release to you," Pilate asked the crowd, "Jesus Barabbas, or Jesus who is called the Messiah?" (27:17). Yes, you read that correctly. Both men were named Jesus.

Now that we've identified the crime Barabbas committed and the meaning of his name, we can move on to discuss the implications of these insights.

Lesson 2: To embrace Jesus' way of making peace, Christlike peacemakers must reject the Barabbas alternative.

Throughout Holy Week, two competing ways of making peace collide. And now, as two rival messiahs stand before us, we must choose between the two approaches to peacemaking they represent. This is the fundamental decision confronting us on Good Friday. As Brian Zahnd summarizes the options: "Jesus of Nazareth calls us to the way of peace by loving our enemies and the practice of radical forgiveness. Jesus Barabbas is willing to fight our wars and kill our enemies in the name of freedom."[9]

All Christians claim to embrace Jesus as their Lord and Savior. But the great tragedy in the church—ever since the time of Constantine—is that many have unknowingly embraced the wrong Jesus. They are clinging with all their might to Jesus Barabbas as they refuse to let go of his way of making peace. Said another way, if we approve of our country killing enemies and using force to advance its national interests, then we have in effect chosen Barabbas and rejected Jesus.

I admit this is a strong statement. But softening this point would intentionally obscure one of the main lessons the gospel writers are trying to teach us on Good Friday: namely, we cannot have it both ways. If we choose the Barabbas way of making peace, we have rejected Jesus. And conversely, to embrace the Jesus way of making peace, we must reject the Barabbas alternative. That these two options are mutually exclusive becomes abundantly clear as Jesus' trial continues.

THE CRUCIFIXION

When Pilate asked the crowd to choose between Barabbas and Jesus, they immediately chose the one who had proven he was willing to fight for their liberation. "'What shall I do, then, with the one you call the king of the Jews?' Pilate asked them. 'Crucify him!' they shouted. 'Why? What crime has he committed?' asked Pilate. But they shouted all the louder, 'Crucify him!'" (Mark 15:12–14).

All four gospels state that Pilate wanted to release Jesus. He found no basis for the charges brought against Jesus (cf. Matthew 27:23; Mark 15:14; Luke 23:4, 14–16; John 19:4). And he knew the chief priests had handed Jesus over out of self-interest (Mark 15:10). Yet two factors ultimately led Pilate to relent and agree to crucify Jesus. First, the religious leaders had effectively stirred up the crowd, and Pilate now feared that unless he agreed to their demands, "a riot was beginning" (Matthew 27:24 NRSV). Second, the gospel of John tells us that in response to Pilate's repeated attempts to release Jesus, the Jewish leaders cried out, "If you let this man go, you are no friend of Caesar. Anyone who claims to be a king opposes Caesar" (John 19:12). "Friend of Caesar"—*amicus Caesaris* in Latin—was a technical title reserved for official representatives of the emperor. Thus, the Jewish leaders were threatening to inform Caesar if Pilate let a rival king off the hook, a move that would likely result in Pilate being stripped of his post. As a result of this veiled threat, Pilate yielded and sentenced Jesus to be crucified.

Upon receiving the order to crucify Jesus, Pilate's soldiers took him into the palace grounds, where they tortured and mocked him (Mark 15:16–20). Then, as Rome often did with defeated foes, the soldiers paraded Jesus through the streets, eventually leading him out of Jerusalem and to a public execution site known as Golgotha—the place of the skull. Once there, they crucified Jesus along with two rebels on either side of him.

In his book on the cross, missiologist H. R. Weber offers his readers a detailed description of the practice of crucifixion:

> At the place of execution there usually already stood a pole. . . . The convict was then laid on the ground, both

forearms or wrists were tied or nailed to the transverse bar, and he was then raised by the patibulum. . . . Usually, the [vertical] pole measured no more than about seven feet. This meant that wild animals could tear the crucified man apart. The feet of the victims were not supported by a footrest as Christian art has depicted it since the seventh century, but were tied or nailed to the pole. Usually, the condemned man "sat" on a peg which was fixed to the middle of the pole. . . . Generally, the crucified one died of gradual asphyxiation.[10]

In order to detail the act of crucifixion, H. R. Weber had to draw from sources beyond the New Testament. That's because, as Catholic theologian Ronald Rolheiser notes, "all four Gospels take pains to *not* focus on the physical sufferings of Jesus [upon the cross]."[11] Mark, for example, simply writes, "And they crucified him" (Mark 15:24). Matthew, Luke, and John are equally brief in their descriptions (cf. Matthew 27:35; Luke 23:33; John 19:18).

What the gospel writers do focus on, however, is how Jesus responded once nailed to the cross. The Gospels record seven different statements that Jesus made from the cross. For example, he told the repentant rebel crucified next to him, "Today you will be with me in paradise" (Luke 23:43). To his mother, he said, "Woman, here is your son," and to the disciple standing next to her, "Here is your mother" (John 19:26–27). At one point, he declared, "I am thirsty" (John 19:28). And before bowing his head and breathing his last—instead of despairing, "I am finished," or calling for retaliation, "Finish them off"— Jesus cried out, "It is finished" (John 19:30). That is to say, the task is complete. Mission accomplished.

Of Jesus' seven final statements, I want to focus on two. Taking them out of order, let's begin by discussing what is traditionally considered the fourth statement Jesus made on the cross.

Forsaken by God?

Mark writes that roughly six hours after being crucified, Jesus cried out, "'*Eloi, Eloi, lema sabachthani?*' (which means 'My God, my God, why have you forsaken me?')" (15:34).

Many of us were taught in church that because God is holy, God cannot look upon sin. And since, on the cross, Jesus took all our sins upon himself, God the Father turned his face away. God literally abandoned his Son. While this may appear to be the clear meaning of Jesus' statement, such an interpretation is problematic for multiple reasons.

First, having gained a more comprehensive understanding of Jesus' mission, we now know that God is like Jesus. When a sinner comes to Jesus, nowhere in the Gospels do we find Jesus covering his eyes and ordering his disciples to remove the unclean wretch from his presence. On the contrary, over and over again in the Gospels, Jesus sought out sinners, befriended sinners, even dined with sinners. And when the Pharisees acted as if holy living required one to stay away from sinners, Jesus rebuked them. If our understanding of the cross makes God the Father look like the Pharisees and not like Jesus, then we need to reevaluate our theology.

Second, if God literally abandoned Jesus on the cross, why did Jesus keep talking to him? Three of Jesus' seven statements from the cross were addressed to his heavenly Father. Either Jesus forgot that God was no longer with him or he knew that despite *feeling* forsaken, the God who promised to never leave us or forsake us remained by his side (see Deuteronomy 31:6). If God truly abandoned Jesus, then—like a trust fall gone horribly wrong—when Jesus spoke his final words, "Father, into your hands I commit my spirit" (Luke 23:46) and then leaned back into death, no one was there to catch him.

Third, and most compelling of all, is the insistence from the psalm Jesus quoted that God did not forsake him. The words "My God, my God, why have you forsaken me?" are the opening line of Psalm 22. It's a hymn that speaks of immense suffering. In it, the psalmist writes of his hands and feet being pierced (v. 16), his clothes being divided up by his persecutors (v. 18), and his mouth being dry (v. 15). By reciting the opening line, Jesus was saying either that this psalm was about him or that he could relate to the agony experienced by the psalmist. Either way, Jesus was identifying with Psalm 22.

Hanging on the cross, struggling to take each breath, Jesus could not recite the entire psalm. But surely he would want us to take the whole psalm into consideration when interpreting his words. Not doing so would be like if I sang the opening line of the hymn, "Low in the grave he lay, Jesus, my Savior," and you went on to develop an entire fatalistic theology around those words all while neglecting to consider the chorus: "Up from the grave he arose, with a mighty triumph o'er his foes!"

Yes, in his immense suffering, Jesus *felt* abandoned by God, just as the psalmist did. But keep reading the psalm, for it contains a surprise ending: "For [the LORD] has not despised or scorned the suffering of the afflicted one; *he has not hidden his face from him* but has listened to his cry for help" (Psalm 22:24, emphasis added).

Where was God the Father as Jesus hung on the cross? God was right there with him. How can we know this for sure? Because on top of all the reasons I've already given, Jesus said as much mere hours before his crucifixion. "A time is coming and in fact has come," he told his disciples on Thursday evening, "when you will be scattered, each to your own home. You will leave me all alone. Yet I am not alone, for my Father is with me" (John 16:32). It is true that Jesus was abandoned on the cross. But not by God. The disciples were the ones who deserted Jesus in his hour of need.

The first words from the cross

Let's now turn our attention to the first words Jesus spoke from the cross. When we nailed Jesus to a tree, what do you think was the first thing he thought to say? How did he instinctively respond? If I got nailed to a cross, apart from screaming in agony, I would curse my executioners or defend my innocence. But that's not how Jesus responded. Instead, when we crucified Jesus, the true essence of his character spilled out for all to see. "Father, forgive them," Jesus said, "for they do not know what they are doing" (Luke 23:34).

In these dying words, we discover just how radically different Jesus was from the kind of messiah everyone wanted him to be. In fact, I believe the full significance of Jesus' dying words can be grasped only when viewed in contrast with the dying words that sparked the Maccabean revolt two hundred years earlier. We've discussed this event to varying degrees throughout the book, but it's important to recap its broad contours once more:

In 167 BC, the Seleucid Empire desecrated the temple, and soon after, an ailing priest named Mattathias said to his five sons, "Avenge the wrong done to your people. Pay back the Gentiles in full" (1 Maccabees 2:67–68 NRSV). These dying words inspired his son Judas to launch a violent revolt against the Seleucids. And as you'll recall, because of his success in battle, Judas earned the nickname Maccabeus, which means "the hammer."

On Palm Sunday, we saw how the crowd's actions signified that they thought Jesus was coming in the likeness of Judas Maccabeus to bring a hammer down on the Romans. But by Friday morning, as Jesus stood without an ounce of fight in him before Pontius Pilate, the crowds finally realized that Jesus had no intention of wielding a hammer on their behalf.

That is to say—for here we are meant to see ourselves in the crowd—when we realized that Jesus was not the Hammer of God, we chose someone with a proven track record of bringing a hammer down on our enemies (Barabbas), and then we picked up a hammer and we crucified Jesus. In other words, the camp speaker got it all wrong. God is not like a hammer. We are.

And when we nailed Jesus to a cross, his dying words could not have been more different from those of Mattathias. Jesus did not cry out, "Father, avenge the wrong done to me. Pay back these wicked sinners in full!" On the contrary, instead of demanding vengeance, Jesus called for its opposite: "Father, forgive them, for they do not know what they are doing" (Luke 23:34).

Because we know God is like Jesus, we can rest assured that Jesus did not speak these words in hopes of persuading an otherwise reluctant heavenly Father to forgive us. Jesus was not begging God to be merciful. He was not pleading for his Father to refrain from unleashing divine wrath on us. Rather, when Jesus cried out, "Father, forgive them," we can be confident that forgiving us is precisely what God desired to do. As Brian Zahnd writes, "The cross is not what God inflicts upon Jesus in order to forgive, but what God in Christ endures as he forgives. The cross is where the sin of the world coalesced into a hideous singularity so that it might be forgiven en masse."[12]

Lesson 3: Instead of retaliating in kind, Christlike peacemakers break the cycle of violence by forgiving.

On the cross, we unleashed all our fury and hatred onto Jesus, and in return, having endured our wrath and absorbed our sin into himself, Jesus responded with radical forgiveness. Here we see the culmination of how Jesus makes peace. Instead of responding in kind when wronged, Jesus forgave. And in so doing, he revealed a way to break free from the endless cycle of violence and counter-violence that plagues our world.

Because we know Jesus' mission involved showing us how to live, we cannot sideline Jesus' call to forgive by classifying it as solely something he did for us. Rather, when Jesus spoke a much-needed word of forgiveness from the cross, he modeled what it looks like for us to live by a spirit of mercy. As practitioners of Jesus' approach to peacemaking, we too must be willing to forgive those who wrong us.

Having said all that, this peacemaking lesson requires a disclaimer: Forgiveness must never be a cop-out for letting injustice continue unabated. This lesson does not mean, for example, that we tell abused women they must forgive the men who mistreat them. After all, on Wednesday we saw Jesus passionately defend a harassed woman when the disciples berated her. Nor does this lesson mean we repeatedly let oppressors off the hook so they can continue hurting others. After all, on Monday we saw Jesus call out the money changers and animal sellers for the ways they oppressed the poor.

Rather, we forgive because it breaks the cycle of violence. And we forgive because, as Jesus acknowledged on the cross, some people do evil out of ignorance. And ultimately, we forgive because, on the cross, God in Christ forgave us.

THE END?

At three in the afternoon, Jesus cried out in a loud voice, "It is finished," followed by, "Father, into your hands I commit my spirit." With that, he bowed his head, breathed his last, and gave up his spirit. "At that moment," Matthew writes, "the curtain of the temple was torn in two from top to bottom. The earth shook, the rocks split, and the tombs broke open" (27:51–52).

That evening, Joseph of Arimathea—a member of the Sanhedrin who had dissented to the group's decision to kill Jesus—went to Pilate and asked for Jesus' body. Having received permission, "Joseph took the body, wrapped it in a clean linen cloth, and placed it in his own new tomb" (Matthew 27:59–60). Then, as the last glimmers of light faded from the evening sky, a large stone was rolled in front of the tomb's entrance. With that, the tragic events of Good Friday came to a close, and with it the end of another failed messiah.

At least, that is the conclusion everyone reached at the time.

The thing about forgiveness, however, is that it has an uncanny ability to create a future when none seems possible.

8

Saturday and Sunday

Peace Be with You

The next day, the one after Preparation Day, the chief priests and the Pharisees went to Pilate. "Sir," they said, "we remember that while he was still alive that deceiver said, 'After three days I will rise again.' So give the order for the tomb to be made secure until the third day. Otherwise, his disciples may come and steal the body and tell the people that he has been raised from the dead. This last deception will be worse than the first."

"Take a guard," Pilate answered. "Go, make the tomb as secure as you know how." So they went and made the tomb secure by putting a seal on the stone and posting the guard.

—Matthew 27:62–66

The women who had come with Jesus from Galilee followed Joseph and saw the tomb and how his body was laid in it. Then they went home and prepared spices and perfumes. But they rested on the Sabbath in obedience to the commandment.

—Luke 23:55–56

How could the disciples have been so naive, wasting three years of their lives following after yet another self-proclaimed messiah? Sure, Jesus seemed different. They thought he was the real deal. But they had seen others claim to be God's long-awaited messiah, and they knew how the story ended: how it always ended.

In 4 BC, for example, a former slave of Herod the Great, Simon of Perea, claimed to be the messiah. Rome beheaded him. Around the same time a lowly shepherd named Athronges alleged divine anointing in his quest to liberate the Jewish people. He was lucky. He lasted a whole year before getting crushed by Rome. Another messianic pretender, Judas the son of Hezekiah, had some initial success. He managed to dispel the Romans from Sepphoris, a town located just four miles north of Nazareth. His success, however, only increased Rome's resolve to defeat him. In response, Rome burned the town to the ground, sold its inhabitants into slavery, and crucified two thousand of Judas's followers, leaving their bodies to hang on the side of the road like billboards advertising a rebel's fate. And finally, ten years later, there was Judas the Galilean. He inspired thousands to join his cause, but as Acts 5:37 reveals, he too was put to death.

Yes, the disciples should have known better than to place their trust in yet another messianic hopeful touting divine backing and promising change. After all, as N. T. Wright notes, "Nothing had changed. Another young leader had been brutally liquidated. . . . Caesar was on his throne. Death, as usual, had the last word."[1]

The gospel writers say very little about Saturday of Holy Week. Matthew reports that the chief priests and Pharisees petitioned Pilate to place a guard at Jesus' tomb (27:62–66). And Luke briefly states that after making preparations on Friday evening for Jesus' burial, the women who had followed Jesus from Galilee rested on Saturday since it was the Sabbath (23:56). That's it. That's the full extent of what the Gospels tell us about Holy Saturday.

Despite the day's relative silence, the Gospels still provide us with a window into the hearts and minds of the disciples during the time in between Jesus' death and their learning of his resurrection. John states that the disciples spent Sunday (and presumably Saturday) gathered together, hiding in a locked room "for fear of the Jewish leaders" (20:19). Luke adds that as soon as the Sabbath ban on travel had passed, two followers of Jesus hightailed it out of Jerusalem, doubtless to distance themselves from the authorities. Their faces were downcast, we are told, as they spoke of their hope for Israel's liberation dying with Jesus on Friday (24:13–21).

When we read the Gospels, the time between Jesus' death and resurrection passes by in a flash. Yet Saturday must have felt like an eternity for the disciples. Hiding all day in a locked room, they had nothing else to do but sit with their emotions. And after the trauma of the past two days, numerous strong emotions were certainly raging inside of them: Guilt for having abandoned Jesus. Despair that the person they had placed their hope in was dead. Confusion as they struggled to understand why Jesus never put up a fight. And perhaps strongest of all: fear. Fear that the Jewish leaders and Roman authorities would hunt them down. Fear that they would soon succumb to the same fate as Jesus.

HE DESCENDED INTO HELL

So far, we've focused on what the disciples were doing during the time between Jesus' death and their learning of his resurrection. But what does the Bible say that Jesus was doing—as strange as that may sound—while his body lay in the tomb? According to Matthew, when Jesus died on Friday, "The earth shook, the rocks split and the tombs broke open. The bodies of many holy people who had died were raised to life. They came out of the tombs after Jesus' resurrection" (27:51–53). First Peter adds that after "[Jesus] was put to death in the body . . . he went and made proclamation to the imprisoned spirits" (3:18–19).

These verses allude to what theologians call Jesus' descent into hell, or the harrowing of Hades. Protestant Reformers, like John Calvin, spoke passionately about the importance of Christ's descent in their writings.[2] Yet surprisingly, most Protestant churches today say very little on the subject. In fact, the only time you'll hear the descent mentioned in many churches is when they recite the Apostles' Creed: "I believe . . . in Jesus Christ . . . [who] suffered under Pontius Pilate, was crucified, died and was buried; *he descended into hell*; on the third day he rose again from the dead."

Despite the inattention it receives in many Christian circles today, Jesus' descent was of immense importance to the first Christians. For example, in the earliest surviving collection of Christian hymns—known as the *Odes of Solomon*—the climactic final song focuses on the liberation of those in hell. Written with Jesus himself as the speaker, it contains such lines as

Sheol saw me and was shattered,
    and Death ejected me and many with me. . . .
Those who had died ran toward me. . . . .

And I placed my name upon their head,
because they are free and they are mine.[3]

References to the harrowing of hell are not just found in early Christian hymns and poetry. As John Calvin observed, "There is no one of the [early church] fathers who does not mention in his writings Christ's descent into hell."[4] Two examples will suffice:

In the second century, Bishop Melito of Sardis delivered a homily on Holy Saturday in which he imagined Jesus proclaiming to hell's captives: "I order you, O sleeper, to awake. I did not create you to be held a prisoner in hell. Rise from the dead, for I am the life of the dead. Rise up, work of my hands, you who were created in my image. Rise, let us leave this place, for you are in me and I am in you."[5]

Two centuries later, Cyril of Alexandria penned a stirring reflection on the cosmic ramifications of Christ's descent. "When he shed his blood for us," Cyril wrote, "Jesus Christ destroyed death and corruptibility. . . . For if he had not died for us, we should not have been saved, and if he had not gone down among the dead, death's cruel empire would never have been shattered."[6]

Murals and mosaics throughout Eastern Christendom beautifully depict Cyril's last line about the shattering of death's cruel empire. The most stunning of these images is arguably the *Anastasis*, painted on the ceiling of the Chora Church (now the Chora Museum) in Istanbul. It depicts Jesus clothed in white, standing atop the shattered gates of hell, with Satan bound at his feet. Unlike Protestant artwork of the resurrection, which tends to depict only Jesus rising from the dead, the *Anastasis* shows Jesus pulling Adam and Eve out of their opened sarcophagi as together they lead a procession of liberated souls out of hell.

Lesson 1: Christlike peacemakers endure the darkest of days, trusting that God is at work even when God appears absent.

For the purposes of this book, we don't need to develop an in-depth theology of Holy Saturday. Besides, given the limited biblical material on the day, such a task would likely produce more questions than answers. What we can glean from the Bible about Holy Saturday, however, is an important peacemaking lesson. For you see, when you contend for peace in places where it is painfully absent, most days feel like Holy Saturday: silent, confusing, hopeless.

Peacemaking can be hard, discouraging work. The destructive forces plaguing our communities often seem unstoppable. Yet even on days when all hope feels lost, Saturday reminds us that Jesus is at work, robbing the grave and plundering even the darkest of hells. This lesson does not mean we deny the reality of death and suffering around us. Rather, Holy Saturday gives us the courage to remain immersed in such realities.

In other words, on days when God appears absent and it feels as if the principalities and powers of this world have won, Holy Saturday reminds us to press on. Press on, for Jesus is at work beneath the surface, defeating death and dismantling despair. Press on, for the days when Jesus seems most lifeless may actually be the days when he's most actively working for our peace. And above all, press on, for Sunday is coming.

RESURRECTION SUNDAY

> On the first day of the week, very early in the morning, the women took the spices they had prepared and went to the tomb. They found the stone rolled away from the tomb, but when they entered, they did not find the body of the Lord Jesus. While they were wondering about this, suddenly two men in clothes that gleamed like lightning stood

beside them. In their fright the women bowed down with their faces to the ground, but the men said to them, "Why do you look for the living among the dead? He is not here; he has risen! Remember how he told you, while he was still with you in Galilee: 'The Son of Man must be delivered over to the hands of sinners, be crucified and on the third day be raised again.'" Then they remembered his words.

When they came back from the tomb, they told all these things to the Eleven and to all the others. It was Mary Magdalene, Joanna, Mary the mother of James, and the others with them who told this to the apostles. But they did not believe the women, because their words seemed to them like nonsense. Peter, however, got up and ran to the tomb. Bending over, he saw the strips of linen lying by themselves, and he went away, wondering to himself what had happened.

—Luke 24:1–12

Early Sunday morning, Mary Magdalene, Joanna, Mary the mother of James, and at least two other women headed to Jesus' tomb to apply burial spices to his body. Customarily, a corpse was prepared with such spices before being placed in a tomb. But the women ran out of time on Friday since Jesus died in the afternoon, it took until that evening to acquire a tomb for him, and soon after—at sundown—the Sabbath began. When the women arrived at the tomb on Sunday morning, they found the stone rolled away and Jesus' body no longer inside (Luke 24:2–3). One can only imagine the mix of panic, confusion, and heartbreak that the women must have felt as they struggled to make sense of the situation. Had somebody stolen Jesus' body? If so, what did they do with it? And if not, what other explanation could there be?

Luke states that the women "were wondering about this" when two men gleaming like lightning appeared (24:4).

"Why do you look for the living among the dead?" the divine messengers asked. "He is not here; he has risen!" (vv. 5–6). Astonished, the women left the tomb and rushed to the secret location where the disciples and other followers of Jesus were hiding from the authorities. Once there, they told everyone the good news, and in so doing these women became the first evangelists, the first to preach the Easter message that Jesus had risen from the dead.

Despite there being at least five eyewitnesses to corroborate the account, the disciples dismissed the women's testimony as sheer nonsense. This invites the question: Was it the *testimony* or the *testifiers* that these men found so hard to believe? Most likely, the answer was both. In the ancient world, the testimony of women was deemed weak and unreliable. In a court of law, for instance, women were not considered credible witnesses. Because the disciples had grown up in this misogynistic culture, this likely influenced their decision to dismiss the women's report.

That said, it's important that we also understand why the testimony itself seemed nonsensical to the disciples. For you see, it's not that first-century Jews didn't believe in the idea of a future resurrection. Many did. But no first-century Jew associated the resurrection with the messiah. As N. T. Wright explains, the resurrection "was to be a great final event in which all God's people would be raised from the dead in the end. It would be the launching point of God's new world, his new creation, the 'age to come.' It would happen to *all* God's people in the *end*, not to one person inconveniently and out of sequence (as it were) in the middle of history, with all the muddle and mess of the world still going on around it."[7]

The disciples rejected the women's testimony in part because it contradicted their understanding of how the resurrection was supposed to unfold. They expected the resurrection to take place at the end of time, when death would be defeated and God's kingdom would be established over all the earth.

The disciples and other first-century Jews may have gotten the timing wrong, but at least they grasped a central truth about the resurrection that we often forget: namely, that the resurrection signified the beginning of the future promised by God. To put it differently, with the raising of Jesus, God's future had begun to break in to the present world order. And as we turn our attention now to the final scene of Easter Sunday, we'll find Jesus enlisting his followers to help make that future a present reality.

Commissioned to make peace

> On the evening of that first day of the week, when the disciples were together, with the doors locked for fear of the Jewish leaders, Jesus came and stood among them and said, "Peace be with you!" After he said this, he showed them his hands and side. The disciples were overjoyed when they saw the Lord.
>
> Again Jesus said, "Peace be with you! As the Father has sent me, I am sending you." And with that he breathed on them and said, "Receive the Holy Spirit. If you forgive anyone's sins, their sins are forgiven; if you do not forgive them, they are not forgiven."
>
> —John 20:19–23

Can you imagine what was running through the disciples' minds when Jesus first appeared to them on Sunday evening? I'm no fan of horror movies, but I've seen enough of their trailers to know that the plot often involves someone coming back from the dead to exact revenge on those who betrayed them. Since we weren't the ones personally betrayed, it's easy for us to move past the fact that this is precisely what the disciples did to Jesus the last time they were together. They betrayed him, abandoned him, denied knowing him, and left him for dead. So it's understandable that, as Luke tells us, the disciples were "startled and frightened" when Jesus suddenly materialized inside their locked hideout (24:37).

Yet instead of exacting revenge or shouting "Curses be upon you!," the first words to proceed from Jesus' mouth were "Peace be with you!" (John 20:19). Once again, Jesus astounds us with his mercy. As John Dear notes, "There's not a trace of anger, resentment, retaliation or vengeance. There's no argument, no 'I told you so,' no condemnation."[8] Rather, Jesus spoke a healing word that calmed his disciples' fears and invited them back into community with him. Immediately after speaking this much-needed word of peace over his disciples, Jesus showed them the wounds on his hands and side.

Then, in the closing moments of Easter Sunday, Jesus commissioned his disciples to continue the peacemaking work for which he was sent into the world. He began by saying for a second time, "Peace be with you," only this time the words function not as a greeting but rather as the fulfillment of the promise he made on Thursday evening: "Peace I leave with you; my peace I give to you," he told his disciples in the upper room. "In this world you will have trouble. But take heart! I have overcome the world" (John 14:27; 16:33). For the disciples, who had just observed the wounds on Jesus' hands and side, it was now unmistakably clear how Jesus overcame the world. He did so not by military might, but through self-giving love. "This is how I make peace," Jesus said in effect. "And now this peace is yours. Yours to experience personally and to extend proactively."

Which is why Jesus used his very next breath to declare, "As the Father has sent me, I am sending you" (John 20:21). Again, we are reminded that Jesus is the one we are called to imitate. We are his ambassadors, sent out into the world to continue the peacemaking mission for which God sent Jesus into the world. Everywhere we go, we are to proclaim God's peace and labor to make it a reality.

Thankfully, we are not expected to carry out this mission on our own. Rather, as soon as Jesus commissioned his disciples, he then breathed on them and said, "Receive the Holy Spirit." And then, in the final words of Easter Sunday, Jesus revealed the primary power that the Holy Spirit bestows upon us. It is not—as many throughout history have assumed—the power to be victorious in battle, or the strength to exact revenge on one's enemies. Quite the opposite. According to Jesus, as we go out into the world as his ambassadors for peace, the Holy Spirit will empower us to extend God's forgiveness to others. Put simply, forgiveness is our superpower.

Lesson 2: Christlike peacemakers cultivate the future promised by Jesus.

When Mattathias lay on his deathbed and instructed his five sons to "avenge the wrong done to your people. Pay back the Gentiles in full" (1 Maccabees 2:67–68 NRSV), his dying words sparked a violent revolution. Two hundred years later, when Jesus hung on a cross and cried out, "Father, forgive them, for they do not know what they are doing" (Luke 23:34), his dying words also sparked a revolution, though this revolution would be nonviolent in nature.

In his book *The Day the Revolution Began*, N. T. Wright states, "The cross was the moment when something *happened* as a result of which the world became a different place, inaugurating God's future plan. The revolution began then and there; Jesus' resurrection was the first sign that it was indeed under way."[9]

The early Christians believed that Jesus' resurrection signified the inbreaking of God's future plans into our present world order. And they taught that in the locked room on Easter Sunday, Jesus commissioned his followers to help make that future a present reality. Every day was to be lived in light of the resurrection. And the church was to serve in this world as an outpost of God's future kingdom.

"We live in a future already bursting upon us," Donald Kraybill writes in his book *The Upside-Down Kingdom*.[10] Or, as Scot McKnight explains in his commentary on the Sermon on the Mount, "Since the kingdom is already making itself present, . . . we are called to live now in light of that future consummation."[11]

In the church I attend, we recently recited a liturgical prayer that included the line "We pray for a world in which our young people no longer have to sign up to fight." As soon as we read the line, it didn't sit right with me. But it took a moment to realize why. After all, the sentiment behind the prayer is to be commended. Who doesn't long for a world where all fighting has ceased? Yet where this liturgy errs is in its claim that our young people currently "have to sign up to fight." Sure, the prayer dreams of a future in which this is "no longer" necessary. But what it fails to recognize is that we the church are called to live out that future now.

Perhaps no one has articulated this point better than Justin Martyr. In the mid–second century, he wrote of the global church, "We ourselves were well conversant with war, murder and everything evil, but all of us throughout the whole wide earth have traded in our weapons of war. We have exchanged our swords for plowshares, our spears for farm tools. Now we cultivate the fear of God, justice, kindness, faith and the expectation of the future given to us through the Crucified One."[12]

Why did the early Christians—without a single known exception—exchange their weapons of war for tools that cultivate life? Why did they refuse to fight, even when unjustly persecuted? In other words, why didn't they just keep their weapons, yet pray—as we do—for the day when their young people would "no longer have to sign up to fight"? The answer, according to Justin Martyr, is that the early Christians saw it as their mission to cultivate the future promised by Jesus.

"Easter means God's Great Cleanup of an unjust and violent world has begun," Marcus Borg and John Dominic Crossan write. "All are here and now called to participate in what is now a collaborative eschatology."[13] Said another way, because we know that God promises a future in which there will be no more war or fighting, Christian peacemakers make it their mission to cultivate that future reality in the messiness of the here and now. That is what it means to be a people of the resurrection.

IF ONLY YOU KNEW

As we come now to the end of our journey through Holy Week, it's important for us to remember how it all began. At the start of the week, on that dusty road that descended from the Mount of Olives into Jerusalem, Jesus cried out, "If only you knew the things that make for peace." We often assume that when Jesus spoke this lament, he had his impending death in mind. That is to say, we interpret Jesus' words to mean "If only you knew the things that make for peace, you wouldn't kill me."

That may be part of what Jesus meant when he cried out on Palm Sunday. But what if when Jesus spoke this lament, he was also looking beyond the events of Holy Week? What if, in speaking these words, Jesus was aching for a future in which people *did* know the things that make for peace? In other words, what if Jesus was saying, "If only you knew the things that make for peace, then the endless cycles of violence that plague this world could finally be broken."

Francis of Assisi learned from Jesus the things that make for peace. Such knowledge led him to embark, in 1219, on a dangerous peacemaking mission to Egypt where he pleaded with the crusading Christians to stop slaughtering Muslims. When they refused, Francis marched unarmed across the battlefield and asked to speak with the sultan of Egypt, al-Malik al-Kāmil. The two men spent several days together discussing the teachings of Jesus. And after safely escorting Francis back to the Crusader camp, al-Kāmil is reported to have said, "If all Christians were like this one, there would be no war between us."

Corrie ten Boom learned from Jesus the things that make for peace. As a result, in 1940, when German Christians invaded the Netherlands, her home became a hiding place for Jewish refugees. Through the network of safe houses that her family oversaw, an estimated eight hundred Jews were saved. In 1944, however, the Nazis raided the ten Boom family home and sent Corrie and her sister Betsie to a concentration camp. Betsie died in the camp, but Corrie survived. After the war, Corrie founded a rehabilitation center for concentration camp survivors. And in a stunning act of mercy, she also opened a shelter for unemployed Dutch men who had collaborated with the Germans during the war.

Around the same time, Bishop Kiril of the Bulgarian Orthodox Church learned from Jesus the things that make for peace. As a result, when his government allied with the Nazis and agreed to deport every Bulgarian Jew, Kiril plotted a courageous act of civil disobedience. On March 10, 1943, when the first fifteen hundred Jews were loaded into boxcars to be sent to the Treblinka extermination camp, Bishop Kiril and his congregation marched unarmed to the train. Once there, Kiril pushed his way through the soldiers as he quoted from the book of Ruth: "Where you go I will go, and where you stay I will stay. Your people will be my people and your God my God" (1:16). He then opened one of the boxcar doors and tried to join those being deported, but the soldiers pulled him out. Far from being deterred, Kiril and his congregation then laid down on the tracks and refused to move. This act stirred the conscience of a nation, and in part because of it, not a single Jew was deported from Bulgaria during World War II.

Despite the majority of Christians around them embracing the way of the hammer, Francis of Assisi, Corrie ten Boom, and Bishop Kiril chose the way of the Lamb. They learned from Jesus the things that make for peace. And instead of just sitting on such knowledge, they put it into action.

We also live in a time when the majority of Christians—or perhaps just the most vocal ones—have chosen the way of the hammer. But after journeying together day by day through Holy Week, you now know the things that make for peace. You now know how Jesus makes peace. Which means only one question remains to be answered:

What will you do with this knowledge?

Discussion Questions

NOTE TO LEADERS

Books like this one are best processed in community. To help encourage such reflection, this section contains several discussion questions for each chapter. If your group wants to study this book during Lent, the next section offers a schedule that divides the chapters into weekly readings. Treat the questions in this section as conversation starters. Your group doesn't need to discuss them all, nor must they go through the questions in the order listed.

Begin each gathering with prayer. Then if time permits, before discussing the book, ask people to share how their week has been. Such a question is partly strategic. Members of your group may have strong opinions about the content of this book. After all, peace and violence can be sensitive topics. But if you start each gathering with a question like the one I've suggested, it can help your group see the humanity in each other. As a result, they'll be more inclined to listen with empathy to those with whom they may disagree. Finally, if you discuss all the questions and still have time remaining, read aloud the heading for one of the peacemaking lessons from the chapter and then ask people to share how they might apply that lesson in their everyday lives.

CHAPTER 1
THE KEY TO HOLY WEEK

1. At the start of Holy Week, Jesus cried out, "If only you knew the things that make for peace." When was a time you saw a group or nation pursue peace in a way that made you weep?

2. How do you define peace? What does it mean to be a peacemaker?

3. This chapter claims that Jesus contended for peace on each day of Holy Week. Given what you already know of the week, what are some ways you see Jesus waging peace? Did Jesus say or do anything during the week that seems to run contrary to the way of peace?

4. What is one conflict or injustice that personally affects you or that you care deeply about seeing resolved? Keep this particular conflict or injustice in mind as you read the rest of the book.

5. What is your main takeaway from this chapter?

CHAPTER 2
PALM SUNDAY: OF HAMMERS AND LAMBS

1. How does your church commemorate Palm Sunday? How has this influenced your understanding of the day?

2. What is something new you learned about Palm Sunday from this chapter?

3. Rome used the threat of force to maintain peace in Jerusalem during Passover. What role does force and the threat of force play in your own country's efforts—be they foreign or domestic—to make and maintain peace?

4. Considering the crowd's actions, what kind of messiah did the people expect Jesus to be?

5. How does Jesus' not-so-triumphal entry serve as a corrective to the crowd's expectations of him?

6. On Palm Sunday, Jesus moved toward conflict instead of dabbling in peacemaking from a safe distance. Is there a conflict you've been avoiding? What might it look like for you to move toward that conflict with the goal of cultivating peace?

CHAPTER 3
MONDAY: THE WHIP OF CHRIST

1. Have you seen others use Jesus' cleansing of the
    temple to justify violence? If so, how?

2. Share about a time when you saw a person or group
    try to help someone in need without first assessing
    the situation. What was the outcome? Were their
    efforts helpful?

3. Is there a difference between pacifism and passivism?
    If so, what is it?

4. A quote (often attributed to Blaise Pascal) reads,
    "Men never do evil so completely and cheerfully
    as when they do it from religious conviction." Do
    you agree? How have you seen others justify evil by
    claiming their actions were motivated by "zeal for
    God" or "righteous anger"?

5. Jesus' actions on Monday only temporarily sus-
    pended the temple's exploitative practices. The money
    changers and animal sellers inevitably returned.
    Given that observation, what role do you think
    symbolic actions play in our efforts to make peace?

6. What is something from the chapter you'd like to
    hear the group's thoughts on?

CHAPTER 4
TUESDAY: TRAPS, TRUTH-TELLING, AND TRAITORS

1. "In our passion to lift up the cross," the author writes, "we've accidentally uprooted it from its context and severed it from the life of the One who gives it meaning" (p. 64). When we separate the death of Jesus from the life of Jesus, what are the ramifications?

2. How has a dualistic worldview infected the church in your country? What would it look like for you to live as if everything belongs to God?

3. What are the implications of Jesus' choosing the kingdom of God as his motto?

4. What does the sailing analogy in this chapter teach you about God's love and our experience of it?

5. What woes are the powerless speaking over you? What would it look like to heed their warnings?

6. What is something you want to remember from this chapter?

CHAPTER 5
WEDNESDAY: TWO ROADS DIVERGED, AND I TOOK . . .

1. Caiaphas justified killing Jesus by claiming that his death would prevent an even worse outcome from happening. Have you seen others concoct a fictional future to justify their violent intentions? If so, give an example. Were you convinced by their claims?

2. "If you want to be a practitioner of Jesus' approach to peacemaking," the author writes, "then you must learn to see the means you use as nothing less than the end coming into existence" (p. 104). Do you agree? If so, what are the implications for how you'll go about contending for peace from here on out?

3. Where you stand determines what you see. How should this observation influence the way we assess conflicts and work for peace?

4. If you live in a powerful nation with a massive military, what are two or three practical ways you can seek out the perspective of those on the margins?

5. Christian ethicist Glen Stassen has observed that crushed expectations are a leading reason why people turn to violence. How can this observation inform our strategies for assessing and ending violent conflicts?

6. What is something new you learned from this chapter?

CHAPTER 6
THURSDAY: A COMMUNITY CONCEIVED

1. Tell of a time you experienced the love of Christ in community.

2. The author writes, "Christian peacemakers should strive to form communities that model on a small scale the peace they seek to cultivate on a grand scale" (p. 130). Do you agree? If so, how will this insight change the way you work for peace?

3. The first half of this chapter focuses on the new love command that Jesus gave during the Last Supper. What else can we learn from the Last Supper about Jesus' approach to peacemaking?

4. When it comes to peacemaking, we often focus on individual exemplars of nonviolence like Rosa Parks, Dr. King, and Gandhi. Have you seen any communities model peacemaking well? If so, tell about one such community.

5. On Maundy Thursday, Jesus commanded Peter, "Put your sword back in its place, for all who draw the sword will die by the sword" (Matthew 26:52). What are the implications of this command for Christians today?

6. What stands out to you from this chapter?

CHAPTER 7
FRIDAY: WHO HOLDS THE HAMMER?

1. Jesus had a chance to die like a scapegoat on the Day of Atonement, but he chose instead to lay down his life on Passover. What are the implications of this observation? What role does forgiveness play in God's liberating work?

2. Why is it wrong to say that Jesus saves us from God?

3. Share about someone you know who lives by a spirit of mercy. What effect has this person had on others?

4. One of the boldest statements in the book is, "If we choose the Barabbas way of making peace, we have rejected Jesus. And conversely, to embrace the Jesus way of making peace, we must reject the Barabbas alternative" (p. 155). Do you agree? Share your thoughts with the group.

5. In the aftermath of apartheid in South Africa, Archbishop Desmond Tutu often remarked, "There is no future without forgiveness." What do you think he meant by this? How have you seen forgiveness break the cycle of violence? How have you seen forgiveness used as a cop-out to let injustice continue?

6. What was most memorable for you from this chapter?

CHAPTER 8
SATURDAY AND SUNDAY: PEACE BE WITH YOU

1. What thoughts or feelings did the early Christian teaching on Christ's descent into hell conjure up in you?

2. Peacemaking can be hard, discouraging work. Yet Holy Saturday reminds us to press on even when it feels as if God is absent and hate has won. If you're willing, share about a season in your life that felt like Holy Saturday. Did Sunday ever come? If not yet, how can the group pray and support you during this trying time?

3. Eberhard Arnold, cofounder of the Bruderhof, once wrote, "The church's present character must proclaim its future goal." What do you think he meant by this? How should this shape the way we work for peace?

4. How has your understanding of Holy Week deepened through the reading of this book? How, if at all, has it changed?

5. Now that you've seen how Jesus made peace during Holy Week, what will you do with this knowledge? How will it change the way you contend for peace from here on out?

How to Use This Book during Lent

This book is intended to be read any time of year. After all, the events of Holy Week shape the entire Christian life. Each day, we are called to take up our cross and follow after Jesus. And because of the resurrection, every day is now a mini Easter.

That said, this book is also designed for individuals and groups to use as a Lenten Bible study. In the previous section, discussion questions are included for each chapter. Here is a suggested schedule for use during Lent, with listed chapters to be read beforehand.

First Sunday of Lent	Discuss "The Key to Holy Week" and Palm Sunday chapters. These have a combined length equal to subsequent chapters.
Second Sunday of Lent	Discuss Monday's chapter.
Third Sunday of Lent	Discuss Tuesday's chapter.
Fourth Sunday of Lent	Discuss Wednesday's chapter.
Fifth Sunday of Lent	Discuss Thursday's chapter.
Sixth Sunday of Lent	Discuss Friday's chapter.
Easter Sunday	Discuss the combined Saturday/Sunday chapter.

Acknowledgments

First and foremost, thanks to my wife Laura for believing in me and the message of this book. Your encouragements spurred me on. Your confidence in my writing calmed my doubts. And your suggestions, as I ran countless ideas by you, greatly improved this book.

Thanks also to Kelly Browning, Craig Greenfield, Cindy Dawson, David Bridges, Kristin Jack, Eddy Hall, Dee Porterfield, David and Joyce Byrne, Andrea and David Moses, and Pat Springle. Your feedback on early drafts of each chapter was invaluable. Likewise, thanks to Josiah Brown, Charity Kemper Sandstrom, and Jay McDermond for reading the manuscript before I submitted it. Your input made this a better book.

Margot Starbuck gave crucial feedback on my book proposal. Christi McGuire masterfully edited my sample chapters. And Rachelle Gardner proved to be the exact writing coach I needed. To all three of you, thanks for investing in authors like myself.

I suspect no literary agent has worked harder for her authors than Mary DeMuth. She has been a sage guide, a constant advocate, and a dear friend on the path to publication. Mary, thanks for believing in this book.

And finally, to Amy Gingerich, Laura Leonard, Sara Versluis, Sherah-Leigh Gerber, and the rest of the team at Herald Press, thank you for taking a chance on this first-time author. My own life has been deeply shaped by the writings of many Herald Press authors. It's an honor to now join this family of authors as collectively we strive to point the church to Jesus and his way of making peace.

Notes

PREFACE: THE FAILED PEACEMAKER

1 Quoted in Olivia Ward, "City States Could be Shape of Future," The Toronto Star, June 28, 2007, https://www.thestar.com/news/2007/06/28/city_states_could_be_shape_of_future.html.

CHAPTER 2: PALM SUNDAY: OF HAMMERS AND LAMBS

1 Flavius Josephus, *Antiquities* 17.9.3.
2 Marcus J. Borg and John Dominic Crossan, *The Last Week: What the Gospels Really Teach about Jesus's Final Days in Jerusalem* (New York: HarperOne, 2006), 3.
3 Amy-Jill Levine, *Entering the Passion of Jesus: A Beginner's Guide to Holy Week* (Nashville: Abingdon Press, 2018), 35.
4 On this point, I am indebted to W. R. Farmer, who, as far as I am aware, was the first to call attention to the use of palm branches on the coins struck by the Maccabeans and during the Jewish revolts of AD 66–70 and 135. See Farmer, "The Palm Branches in John 12:13," *Journal of Theological Studies* 3 (1952): 63.

5 This term was first used by Ched Myers to describe Jesus' triumphal entry. See Myers, *Binding the Strong Man: A Political Reading of Mark's Story of Jesus* (Maryknoll: Orbis, 1994), 294.

6 Myers, *Binding the Strong Man*, 295.

7 Pope Benedict XVI, *Jesus of Nazareth: Holy Week: From the Entrance into Jerusalem to the Resurrection* (San Francisco: Ignatius Press, 2011), 3.

8 J. F. Coakley, "Jesus' Messianic Entry into Jerusalem (John 12:12–19 PAR.)," *The Journal of Theological Studies* 46, no. 2 (October 1995): 461.

CHAPTER 3: MONDAY: THE WHIP OF CHRIST

1 Not bound by modern literary constraints, ancient biographers often arranged their material topically instead of chronologically. Defining moments were frequently placed early on, since these events helped explicate all that would follow. Matthew, Mark, and Luke explicitly state that Jesus cleansed the temple during his final week. Most scholars believe that even though his account of the temple cleansing is found near the start of his gospel, John is describing this same event. As New Testament scholar Craig Keener writes, "John opens Jesus' ministry with [this scene] for theological reasons. Now Jesus' entire ministry is the Passion Week, overshadowed by his impending 'hour.'" Keener, *The Gospel of John: A Commentary*, 2 vols. (Grand Rapids, MI: Baker Academic, 2012), 1:519.

2 Daniel Dombrowski, "A Cleansing of the Cleansings: On the Danger Art Poses to Christian Pacifism," *Peace Research* 15, no. 1 (January 1983): 26.

3 Augustine, *Answer to Petilian the Donatist*, 2.10.24; cf. 2.81.178.

4 Bernard of Clairvaux, *In Praise of the New Knighthood*, 5.9.

5 John Calvin, *Defensio Orthodoxae Fidei* (1554). See Andy Alexis-Baker, "Violence, Nonviolence and the Temple Incident in John 2:13–15," *Biblical Interpretation* 20 (2012): 85.

6 Ched Myers, *Binding the Strong Man: A Political Reading of Mark's Story of Jesus* (Maryknoll, NY: Orbis, 1988), 299.

7 While the Greek verb behind this action, *ekballo*, is often translated as "drove out," the word itself does not denote a violent act. For example, Mark 1:12 uses *ekballo* to state that "the Spirit *sent* [Jesus] *out* into the wilderness." Likewise, in Matthew 9:38, Jesus

says to his disciples, "Ask the Lord of the harvest . . . to *send out* workers into his harvest field." In both cases, *ekballo* contains no connotation of force.

8 N. Clayton Croy, "The Messianic Whippersnapper: Did Jesus Use a Whip on People in the Temple (John 2:15)?," *Journal of Biblical Literature* 128, no. 3 (2009): 557.

9 See Croy, 557, for a comprehensive list of the papyri and uncials of John's gospel that include *hōs*.

10 Raymond Brown, *The Gospel according to John I–XII* (Garden City, NY: Doubleday, 1966), 116. See also Alexis-Baker, "Violence, Nonviolence and the Temple Incident," 88.

11 See Keener, *Gospel of John*, 1:521. See also Daniel Izuzquiza, *Rooted in Jesus Christ: Toward a Radical Ecclesiology* (Grand Rapids, MI: Eerdmans, 2009), 233.

12 For those wanting precise grammatical terminology, "*te* [noun] *kai* [noun]" constructions in the Bible function as partitive appositions every time they modify a noun or substantive adjective. A substantive adjective is simply an adjective that stands alone and functions as a noun, such as the word *all* in John 2:15. Appositives define the word they modify. Partitive appositions do this by breaking down the modified noun or substantive adjective into its constituent parts.

13 The complete list of "*te* [noun] *kai* [noun]" phrases modifying a Greek form of *all* is Matthew 22:10; John 2:15; Acts 19:10, 17; 26:3; Romans 1:16, 2:9, 10; 3:9; Hebrews 2:11; James 3:7; Revelation 19:18.

14 Croy, "Messianic Whippersnapper," 561.

15 Brooke Foss Westcott, *Gospel according to St. John* (London: James Clarke, 1958), 41.

16 Alexis-Baker, "Violence, Nonviolence and the Temple Incident," 92.

17 Myers, *Binding the Strong Man*, 290.

18 Scott Bessenecker, *Overturning Tables: Freeing Missions from the Christian-Industrial Complex* (Downers Grove, IL: IVP Books, 2014), 16. See also Keener, *Gospel of John*, 1:524; Josephus, *Against Apion* 2.102–5.

19 Andreas J. Köstenberger, *John* (Grand Rapids, MI: Baker Academic, 2004), 106.

20 Marcus J. Borg and John D. Crossan, *The Last Week: What the Gospels Really Teach about Jesus's Final Days in Jerusalem* (New York: HarperOne, 2006), 44.

21 Mishnah Shekalim 4:4. See also Tosefta Shekalim 1:8.

22 Mishnah Keritot 1:7. For a more detailed discussion of this event, see Joachim Jeremias, *Jerusalem in the Time of Jesus: An Investigation into Economic and Social Conditions during the New Testament Period* (Philadelphia: Fortress, 1969), 33–34.

23 Flavius Josephus, *Antiquities* 20.9.2.

24 Stanley Hauerwas, *Matthew* (Grand Rapids, MI: Brazos, 2015), 184.

25 Pope Benedict XVI, *Jesus of Nazareth: Holy Week: From the Entrance into Jerusalem to the Resurrection* (San Francisco: Ignatius Press, 2011), 40. See also John 2:19.

26 Pope Benedict XVI, 22.

CHAPTER 4: TUESDAY: TRAPS, TRUTH-TELLING, AND TRAITORS

1 Special thanks to N. T. Wright, who first drew my attention to this similarity between Jesus and Judas the Galilean. See Wright, *The Scriptures, the Cross, and the Power of God: Reflections for Holy Week* (Louisville, KY: Westminster John Knox, 2006), 24–25.

2 Marcus J. Borg and John Dominic Crossan, *The Last Week: What the Gospels Really Teach about Jesus's Final Days in Jerusalem* (New York: HarperOne, 2006), 25.

3 In fact, Judas the Galilean's chief partner in his failed tax revolt was a Pharisee named Zadok.

4 Ched Myers, *Binding the Strong Man: A Political Reading of Mark's Story of Jesus* (Maryknoll, NY: Orbis, 1988), 311.

5 Wright, *The Scriptures, the Cross,* 27.

6 See R. T. France, *The Gospel of Matthew* (Grand Rapids, MI: Wm. B. Eerdmans, 2007), 830.

7 France, 380.

8 Wright, *The Scriptures, the Cross,* 26.

9 Borg and Crossan, *The Last Week,* 64.

10 Andreas Köstenberger and Justin Taylor, "The Escalating Conflict," in *Your Sorrow Will Turn to Joy: Morning and Evening Meditations for Holy Week* (Minneapolis, MN: Desiring God, 2016), 35.

11 In fact, the last thing Jesus taught before the Herodians and Pharisees asked him their tax question was that God owns the vineyard; all earthly rulers—though they may claim ownership—are mere tenants (Mark 12:1–12).

12 In this section, I am indebted to Glen Stassen and David Gushee,
    who first drew my attention to the history of how this passage
    came to be interpreted dualistically. See Stassen and Gushee, *King-
    dom Ethics: Following Jesus in Contemporary Context* (Downers
    Grove, IL: InterVarsity Press, 2003), 128–32.

13 Justin Martyr, *First Apology*, 17.

14 I don't doubt the sincerity of Justin's faith. After all, he would later
    be martyred for refusing to give the emperor the one thing Justin
    claimed belonged to God alone—his worship. Nor do I question
    the motivation behind his interpretation. I suspect Justin genuinely
    believed it was what Jesus meant. But that's because, as Stassen
    and Gushee point out, Justin was a Gentile, not a Jew (*Kingdom
    Ethics*, 129). And before his Christian conversion, Justin studied
    the works of Plato, who taught a form of dualism that separated
    the spiritual from the earthly. It's easy to see how this unbiblical
    worldview colored Justin's reading of Jesus' tax answer.

15 Stassen and Gushee, 129.

16 Stassen and Gushee, 129.

17 Stanley Hauerwas, *Matthew* (Grand Rapids, MI: Brazos Press,
    2006), 197.

18 See, for example, R. L. Thomas, *New American Standard
    Hebrew-Aramaic and Greek Dictionaries: Updated Edition*
    (Anaheim, CA: Foundation Publications, 1998); or James Strong,
    The New Strong's Concise Dictionary of Bible Words (Nashville:
    Thomas Nelson, 2000).

19 Alexander Souter, *A Pocket Lexicon to the Greek New Testament*
    (Oxford, UK: Clarendon Press, 1917), 182.

20 Gary Deddo, "The Work of Christ on the Cross" (unpublished
    lecture, Fuller Theological Seminary, Houston, TX, May, 14, 2011).

21 Hauerwas, *Matthew*, 197.

22 Flavius Josephus, *The Jewish War* 5.224

23 Borg and Crossan, *The Last Week*, 75–76.

24 Barbara Brown Taylor, *The Seeds of Heaven: Sermons on the
    Gospel of Matthew* (Louisville, KY: Westminster John Knox,
    2004), 109.

25 Taylor, 109.

26 C. I. Scofield, "The Millennium: A Sermon Preached at the First
    Congregational Church, Dallas, Texas, Oct. 29, 1893," Scofield
    Memorial Church Archives, Dallas; Paul Boyer, *When Time*

Shall Be No More: Prophecy Belief in Modern American Culture (Cambridge, MA: Belknap Press, 1992), 298.

27 A number of scholars have written about the Jewish-Roman war and its relation to Jesus' apocalyptic warning on Holy Tuesday (e.g., Pope Benedict XVI, *Jesus of Nazareth: Holy Week: From the Entrance into Jerusalem to the Resurrection* [San Francisco: Ignatius Press, 2011], 24–52; Hauerwas, *Matthew*, 201–12). But none have written more eloquently or persuasively on the subject than Ched Myers (see *Binding the Strong Man*, 324–53). His thoughts have greatly shaped my own in this section.

28 Myers, *Binding the Strong Man*, 332.

29 Josephus, *The Jewish War* 6.288–99. See also Richard A. Horsley and John S. Hanson, *Bandits, Prophets and Messiahs: Popular Movements in the Time of Jesus* (Minneapolis, MI: Winston Press, 1985), 182–83.

30 Myers, *Binding the Strong Man*, 330.

31 Myers, 331.

32 Myers, 332.

33 Myers, 332.

34 Myers, 337.

35 Pope Benedict XVI, *Jesus of Nazareth*, 30. The event is originally recounted by Josephus in *The Jewish War* 5.6.1.

36 See Eusebius of Caesarea, *Church History* 3.5.3; Epiphanius of Salamis, *Against Heresies* 29.7.8.

37 Hauerwas, *Matthew*, 208.

CHAPTER 5: WEDNESDAY: TWO ROADS DIVERGED, AND I TOOK . . .

1 David Matthis, "Betrayed by One of His Own," in *Your Sorrow Will Turn to Joy: Morning and Evening Meditations for Holy Week* (Minneapolis, MN: Desiring God, 2016), 45.

2 Craig S. Keener, *The Gospel of Matthew: A Socio-Rhetorical Commentary* (Grand Rapids, MI: Eerdmans, 2009), 616. See also Josephus, *Antiquities* 15.173; 20.216–18.

3 Oscar Romero, *The Scandal of Redemption: When God Liberates the Poor, Saves Sinners, and Heals Nations* (Walden, NY: Plough Publishing House, 2018), 65.

4 Brian Zahnd, *The Unvarnished Jesus: A Lenten Journey* (n.p.: Spello Press, 2019), 27.

5 Martin Luther King Jr., *The Trumpet of Conscience* (Boston: Beacon Press, 2011), 73.

6 While Matthew and Mark never reveal the woman's name, the gospel of John identifies her as Mary (see John 12:3).

7 Ben Witherington III, *The Gospel of Mark: A Socio-Rhetorical Commentary* (Grand Rapids, MI: Eerdmans, 2001), 367.

8 David Daube, *The New Testament and Rabbinic Judaism* (Eugene, OR: Wipf and Stock, 2011), 315.

9 Keener, *Gospel of Matthew*, 618.

10 Marcus J. Borg and John Dominic Crossan, *The Last Week: What the Gospels Really Teach about Jesus's Final Days in Jerusalem* (New York: HarperOne, 2006), 104.

11 Taylor Owen and Ben Kiernan, "Roots of U.S. Troubles in Afghanistan: Civilian Bombing Casualties and the Cambodian Precedent," *Asia-Pacific Journal* 8, no. 4 (Summer 2010): 6.

12 Ben Kiernan, *How Pol Pot Came to Power: Colonialism, Nationalism and Communism in Cambodia, 1930–1975* (New Haven, CT: Yale University Press, 2004), xxiii.

13 Central Intelligence Agency, "Efforts of Khmer Insurgents to Exploit for Propaganda Purposes Damage Done by Airstrikes in Kandal Province" (intelligence information cable,) April 20, 1973, declassified February 19, 1987, abstract available at https://library.usask.ca/vietnam/index.php?state=view&id=753.

14 Tyrian shekels weighed 14 grams and had a silver purity of 94 percent. Totaling 12.69 ounces of silver, and with today's silver price of $23.12 per ounce (which is at a five-year high), that equates to a value of $293.39 USD.

15 David E. Garland, *The NIV Application Commentary: Mark* (Grand Rapids, MI: Zondervan, 2011), 522.

16 Michael Radu, "Terrorism after the Cold War: Trends and Challenges," *Orbis* 46, no. 2 (Spring 2002): 286.

17 Alan Krueger and Jitka Malecková, "Education, Poverty and Terrorism: Is There a Causal Connection?," *Journal of Economic Perspectives* 17, no. 4 (Fall 2003): 128–29.

18 Glen H. Stassen, "Just Peacemaking as Hermeneutical Key: The Need for International Cooperation in Preventing Terrorism," *Journal of the Society of Christian Ethics* 24, no. 2 (Fall/Winter 2004): 185.

CHAPTER 6: THURSDAY: A COMMUNITY CONCEIVED

1 Jon Bloom, "Not My Will Be Done," in *Your Sorrow Will Turn to Joy: Morning and Evening Meditations for Holy Week* (Minneapolis, MN: Desiring God, 2016), 63.

2 On this point, I am indebted to Wallace T. Viets, who, as far as I am aware, was the first to suggest that the man carrying a water jar functioned as a prearranged signal. See Viets, *Seven Days That Changed the World* (New York: Abingdon Press, 1962), 61. A number of authors have since expanded on Viets's theory. See James Roy Smith, *His Finest Week* (Nashville: Upper Room, 1971), 39; Ched Myers, *Binding the Strong Man: A Political Reading of Mark's Story of Jesus* (Maryknoll, NY: Orbis Books, 1988), 360–61; Andreas J. Köstenberger and Justin Taylor, *The Final Days of Jesus: The Most Important Week of the Most Important Person Who Ever Lived* (Wheaton, IL: Crossway, 2014), 54.

3 Myers, *Binding the Strong Man*, 361.

4 Thanks to John Dear, whose writings influenced my thinking on this point. See Dear, *Walking the Way: Following Jesus on the Lenten Journey of Gospel Nonviolence to the Cross and Resurrection* (New London, CT: Twenty-Third Publications, 2015), 58.

5 Dear, *Walking the Way*, 58.

6 Frederick Dale Bruner, *The Gospel of John: A Commentary* (Grand Rapids, MI: Eerdmans, 2012), 792.

7 For a more in-depth explanation, see Dave Andrews, *A Divine Society: The Trinity, Community and Society* (Eugene, OR: Wipf and Stock, 2012), 109–10.

8 Joseph A. Grassi, *Jesus Is Shalom: A Vision of Peace from the Gospels* (New York: Paulist Press, 2006), 86.

9 For those interested in learning more about the power of a community, I recommend reading George G. Hunter's classic book *The Celtic Way of Evangelism* (Nashville, TN: Abingdon Press, 2000). Chapters 2 and 4, in particular, unpack how Saint Patrick's community-based approach to evangelism resulted in the rapid spread of Christianity throughout Ireland in the fifth century.

10 Art Toalston, "Falwell's Concealed-Permit Comments Enter Gun Debate," *Baptist Press*, December 7, 2015, https://www.baptistpress.com/resource-library/news/falwells-concealed-permit-comments-enter-gun-debate/.

11 Quoted in John Piper, "Why I Disagree with Jerry Falwell Jr. on Christians and Guns," *Washington Post*, December 22, 2015, https://www.washingtonpost.com/news/acts-of-faith/wp/2015/12/23/john-piper-why-i-disagree-with-jerry-falwell-jr-on-christians-and-guns/.

12 Steven E. Runge, *Discourse Grammar of the Greek New Testament: A Practical Introduction for Teaching and Exegesis* (Peabody, MA: Hendrickson, 2010), 52.

13 John Dear, *Jesus the Rebel: Bearer of God's Peace and Justice* (Lanham, MD: Sheed & Ward, 2000), 158.

14 Grassi, *Jesus Is Shalom*, 87.

15 "'No More of This!' (Why Jesus Armed and Disarmed Peter)," *Brian Zahnd* (blog), August 10, 2018, https://brianzahnd.com/2018/08/no-jesus-armed-disarmed-peter/.

16 Toalston, "Falwell's Concealed-Permit Comments."

17 Moyer Hubbard, "'Let the One Who Has No Sword, Buy One': The Biblical Argument for Gun Control, Part Two," *The Good Book Blog*, February 25, 2014, https://www.biola.edu/blogs/good-book-blog/2014/let-the-one-who-has-no-sword-buy-one-the-biblical-argument-for-gun-control-part-two.

18 Tertullian, *On Idolatry* 19.

19 Justin Martyr, *Dialogue with Trypho*, 110.

20 Dear, *Walking the Way*, 72.

21 Edward Sri, *No Greater Love: A Biblical Walk through Christ's Passion* (West Chester, PA: Ascension Publishing, 2019), 56.

CHAPTER 7: FRIDAY: WHO HOLDS THE HAMMER?

1 Gary Deddo, "The Work of Christ on the Cross" (unpublished lecture, Fuller Theological Seminary, Houston, TX, May 13, 2011).

2 Brian Zahnd, "The Beautiful Catastrophe" (sermon, Word of Life Church, St. Joseph, MO, March 15, 2015), https://wolc.com/watch--listen/sermon-archives/the-beautiful-catastrophe/.

3 In fact, Mary's song—known as the Magnificat—is so subversive that in the twentieth century alone, local authorities in at least three countries (India, Guatemala, and Argentina) banned its public recitation.

4 Devout Jewish groups at the time—like the Qumran community—frequently cited this text as they wrote of their longing for the messiah's arrival.

5 See Mishnah Yoma 6:3–6.
6 David J. Bosch, *Transforming Mission: Paradigm Shifts in Theology of Mission* (Maryknoll, NY: Orbis, 2007), 111.
7 Jerusalem Talmud *Sanhedrin* I 18a. See also Babylonian Talmud *Sanhedrin* 41a; John 18:31.
8 Philo of Alexandria, *Embassy to Gaius*, 300–301.
9 Brian Zahnd, *The Unvarnished Jesus: A Lenten Journey* (n.p.: Spello Press, 2019), 122–23.
10 Hans-Ruedi Weber, *The Cross: Tradition and Interpretation* (Grand Rapids, MI: Eerdmans, 1975), 6.
11 Ronald Rolheiser, *The Passion and the Cross* (Toronto: Novalis, 2015), 6.
12 Zahnd, *Unvarnished Jesus*, 187.

CHAPTER 8: SATURDAY AND SUNDAY: PEACE BE WITH YOU

1 N. T. Wright, *The Day the Revolution Began: Reconsidering the Meaning of Jesus's Crucifixion* (New York: HarperOne, 2016), 3.
2 See John Calvin, *Institutes of the Christian Religion* 2.16.8–12.
3 *Odes of Solomon* 42:11, 15, 20.
4 Calvin, *Institutes of the Christian Religion* 2.16.8.
5 Melito of Sardis, *Homily for Holy Saturday*.
6 Quoted in J. N. D. Kelly, *Early Christian Doctrines* (New York: Harper and Row, 1959), 397–98.
7 Wright, *Day the Revolution Began*, 175.
8 John Dear, *Walking the Way: Following Jesus on the Lenten Journey of Gospel Nonviolence to the Cross and Resurrection* (New London, CT: Twenty-Third Publications, 2015), 116.
9 Wright, *Day the Revolution Began*, 34. Emphasis in the original.
10 Donald B. Kraybill, *The Upside-Down Kingdom* (Scottdale, PA: Herald Press, 2003), 256.
11 Scot McKnight, *Sermon on the Mount*, ed. Tremper Longman (Grand Rapids, MI: Zondervan, 2016), 179.
12 Justin Martyr, *Dialogue with Trypho* 110.3.4.
13 Marcus J. Borg and John Dominic Crossan, *The Last Week: What the Gospels Really Teach about Jesus's Final Days in Jerusalem* (New York: HarperOne, 2006), 208–10.

The Author

Jason Porterfield has made his home in places abandoned by society, from Canada's poorest neighborhood to the slums of Indonesia. His passion is to cultivate God's shalom wherever it is painfully absent and to help churches embrace their peacemaking vocation.

In 2007, Jason joined Servants (ServantsAsia.org), an international network of Christian communities living and ministering among the urban poor. He was a founding member of the Servants team in Vancouver, started a new team in Indonesia, and directed operations in North America through 2015. Jason holds a masters in theology from Fuller Theological Seminary and now lives in his riskiest location yet: next door to his in-laws.

Get a free copy of Jason's ebook *100 Early Christian Quotes on Not Killing* at JasonPorterfield.com. You can also follow him on Facebook (@JasonGPorterfield) and Instagram (@JG_Porterfield), and can email him directly at Jason@Jason-Porterfield.com.